THEMES TO inSPiRE

3

Themes to inSPiRE

3

FOR **KS3**

Steve Clarke

DYNAMIC LEARNING

HODDER EDUCATION
AN HACHETTE UK COMPANY

Although every effort has been made to ensure that website addresses are correct at the time of going to press, Hodder Education cannot be held responsible for the content of any website mentioned in this book. It is sometimes possible to find a relocated web page by typing in the address of the home page for a website in the URL window of your browser.

Hachette UK's policy is to use papers that are natural, renewable and recyclable products and made from wood grown in sustainable forests. The logging and manufacturing processes are expected to conform to the environmental regulations of the country of origin.

Orders: please contact Bookpoint Ltd, 130 Milton Park, Abingdon, Oxon OX14 4SB. Telephone: +44 (0)1235 827720. Fax: +44 (0)1235 400454. Lines are open 9.00a.m.–5.00p.m., Monday to Saturday, with a 24-hour message answering service. Visit our website at www.hoddereducation.co.uk.

© Steve Clarke 2013
First published in 2013 by
Hodder Education,
an Hachette UK company
Carmelite House, 50 Victoria Embankment
London EC4Y 0DZ

Impression number 10 9 8 7
Year 2022 2021 2020 2019

Cover photo: Red maple leaf on white background © Olivier Blondeau/iStockphoto.com
Illustrations by Barking Dog Art and Oxford Designers and Illustrators
Designed in Minion Regular by The Wooden Ark Ltd (Scarborough)
Printed in Dubai

A catalogue record for this title is available from the British Library
ISBN 978 1 444 122114

Contents

1.1 Why are some places special for religious people?

Learning objectives

You will ...
- find out what a pilgrimage is
- understand why pilgrimages are important for religious people
- reflect on places that are special to you.

Most people have places that have special significance for them. You can see some examples on these two pages.

Usually, the place is special because
- it brings back memories of the past
- it is connected with a special person
- there is a story associated with it
- it stirs certain emotions.

If a place is special to someone, they may go back to visit it, possibly at special times of the year. For example, a person may visit the grave of a loved one on the anniversary of his or her death. They may feel that their visit keeps the memory of that person alive, or that it helps them come to terms with the death.

In the same way, religious people visit special places. The places are usually associated with key happenings in the history of their faith, or important people, or even mythological events.

Religious people who go on journeys to special places are called **pilgrims**. The journeys they go on are called **pilgrimages**.

- Pilgrimages account for much of non-business travel around the world, and religious groups and organisations own most of the world's major tourist sites.
- It is estimated that at least 150 million people go on pilgrimages each year.
- The largest gathering of people in history was in 2001, when 70 million Hindus took part in the Kumbh Mela, a pilgrimage to the River Ganges in India.
- The biggest annual pilgrimage is the Hajj, the pilgrimage to Makkah in Saudi Arabia. It is attended by about 2.5 million Muslims each year.

Average numbers of visitors to top tourist attractions in the UK (per year):

Alton Towers, Staffordshire: 2.7 million

British Museum, London: 5.8 million

Stonehenge, Wiltshire: 1 million

1066 Battle of Hastings, Abbey and Battlefield: 136,500

Edinburgh Castle: 1.2 million

London Eye: 3.5 million

Average numbers of pilgrims visiting top pilgrimage sites in the world (per year):

Our Lady of Guadalupe, Mexico (Christian): 20 million

Ayyapa Saranam, India (Hindu): 30 million

Western Wall, Israel (Jewish): 8 million

Amritsar, India (Sikh): 13 million

Lumbini, Nepal (Buddhist): 100,000

Karbala, Iraq (Muslim): 10 million

Why do so many people go on pilgrimages?

For religious people, a pilgrimage is as much about the journey they make with their spiritual feelings as the actual journey from one place to another.

I am going to a place that is important in the history of my religion.

I believe that going on pilgrimage will help me sort out some of the problems in my life.

I feel close to God as a pilgrim.

I believe that God will forgive my sins.

On pilgrimage, I have the opportunity to reflect on my faith.

I want to use the pilgrimage as a fresh start on my spiritual journey through life.

Many people have been healed on pilgrimage, and I hope to be, too.

Pilgrimage takes me away from ordinary life.

It is a requirement of my religion to go on pilgrimage.

I can feel close to my fellow pilgrims as we share our faith.

I am going to the place where my religion started.

Going on pilgrimage is an opportunity to create good karma and pass it on to others.

Knowledge check

1 What is a pilgrimage?
2 Where was the largest gathering of people in history?
3 Which is the biggest annual pilgrimage?
4 Which site is the most visited Jewish pilgrimage site?
5 Give three reasons why a religious person may go on a pilgrimage.

Activity A

1 Think about a place that is important to you or your family.

2 Design a postcard showing the place.

3 On the back of your postcard explain why the place is special. What special memories do you have of it? How does it make you feel? How has the place influenced your life?

Activity B

1 Conduct some research into the Christian pilgrimage to Lourdes and the Muslim hajj.

2 For each, summarise why it is important and what pilgrims do there.

3 Draw up a comparison chart: what is unique about each and what is similar?

Activity C

1 Make a PowerPoint® presentation showing what a pilgrimage is and how pilgrimages differ from tourist holidays.

2 Use some of the quotations in this chapter to help your explanation.

3 Research and include some examples of pilgrimages from different religions.

Activity D

'The egotists may go on pilgrimages to holy rivers, sacred shrines and foreign lands, but they only gather more of the dirt of egotism … Those who are attached to the True One have their filth washed away.'

'Burnt offerings, sacred feasts, intense meditations with the body upside-down, puja, and taking millions of cleansing baths at sacred shrines of pilgrimage: the merits of all these can be obtained by enshrining the Lord within your heart for a fraction of a second.'

1 What do these quotations from the Guru Granth Sahib mean? First, find out what an egotist is and think about why Sikhism teaches that pilgrimage is egotistical.

2 Why would many followers of religions other than Sikhism disagree?

3 What is your view?

1.2 Why is Israel/Palestine so important?

Learning objectives

You will ...
- find out about pilgrimage sites in Israel/Palestine
- understand why the Holy Land is important to the Abrahamic religions
- analyse why some sites are important to different religions for different reasons.

The land of Israel/Palestine is home to sites of pilgrimage that are important to the three **Abrahamic faiths**: Judaism, Christianity and Islam. Because of this, it is sometimes called the Holy Land.

This map shows the country of Israel. It also shows the areas of land – the West Bank and Gaza – that many people call Palestine.

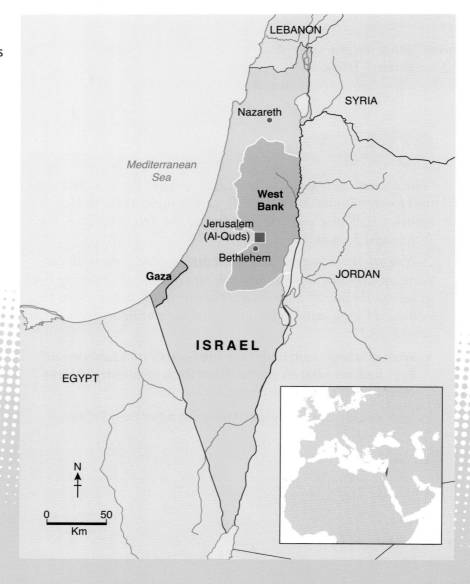

Judaism

For Jews, Israel is the land that God promised them in the time of Abraham, four thousand years ago. The land itself is, therefore, a place of pilgrimage for Jews who don't live there. The city of Jerusalem is Judaism's holiest city. Jews believe that Mount Moriah in Jerusalem is the centre of God's presence on earth.

Tradition says that the Jewish Temple was built on top of Mount Moriah, today known as the Temple Mount. The Temple itself no longer exists, but on the western side of the Temple Mount there is a remnant of one of the Temple walls. It is called the Western Wall. Because of its associations with the Temple and with the Temple Mount, it is the most sacred site in Judaism.

Some people write prayers on paper and place them between the stones of the Wall.

Jews believe that God's presence will never leave the Wall. They gather there to meditate and reflect on their history. It is a place of prayer and tears, and is sometimes called the Wailing Wall. In a way, it is a symbol of the Jewish people: it has never been destroyed, and Jews believe it never will be.

> 'Jerusalem … is much more than a city; it is what binds one Jew to another in a way that remains hard to explain. When a Jew visits Jerusalem for the first time, it is not the first time: it is a homecoming … Its sadness and its joy are part of our collective memory.'
>
> Elie Wiesel, Jewish writer

Christianity

There are many sites in Israel/Palestine associated with the life of Jesus.

Bethlehem

Bethlehem is the town in which people believe Jesus was born, so many Christian pilgrims visit it at Christmas time. They worship at the Basilica of the Nativity in Manger Square, which contains a grotto where Jesus is supposed to have been born.

Galilee

Jesus spent most of his life in an area of northern Israel called Galilee. In 2009, the Jesus Trail was marked out, connecting many of the places associated with Jesus' life. Christians who walk the 65 kilometres believe it gives them a more personal connection with the life of Jesus.

Jerusalem

Jesus spent the last week of his life in Jerusalem and was crucified there. Christians believe that he rose from death three days later. Many pilgrims walk the Via Dolorosa (the Way of Sorrow), the 500-metre route that Jesus took to his execution. It ends at the Church of the Holy Sepulchre, where Jesus is believed to have died and been buried.

Islam

Muslims believe that, by a miracle, Prophet Muhammad was transported one night from Makkah to Jerusalem. There, he was set down on the Temple Mount and led prayers. He was taken from there up to heaven. The rock on which these events are believed to have occurred is covered by the golden Dome of the Rock. Near it is the Al-Aqsa mosque, which commemorates Muhammad's Night Journey.

Muslims call Jerusalem **Al-Quds**, which means 'The Holy', and the Temple Mount is Haram esh-Sharif, meaning 'Noble Sanctuary'. Every Friday, the Al-Aqsa mosque overflows with worshippers wanting to pray at this holy site.

Some Christians carry a cross, as Jesus did, along the Via Dolorosa.

'The mind will be filled with the awesome wonder of so many sacred shrines and this will be cemented in the heart never to fade.'
(William Johnston, Christian writer, writing about a pilgrimage to the Holy Land)

This is the rock from which Muhammad is believed to have been taken up to heaven. It is inside the Dome of the Rock.

Knowledge check

1 Why is Israel/Palestine sometimes called the Holy Land?
2 Why is Mount Moriah important for Jews?
3 What do Jews do at the Western Wall?
4 Where did Jesus spend most of his life?
5 What does the Church of the Holy Sepulchre mark?
6 What is inside the Dome of the Rock?
7 What do Muslims call Jerusalem?

Activity A

1 Make a magazine advertisement for a travel company to attract pilgrims to the Holy Land.
2 Include a map of Israel/Palestine with important pilgrimage sites marked on it. You could colour-code them to connect them to the different religions.
3 Provide information in your advertisement about the sites and include some pictures.
4 You might find out about other pilgrimage sites not mentioned in this chapter.

Activity B

1 Find out more about the Church of the Holy Sepulchre and its history.
2 Find out also about how different Christian groups share responsibility for this church.
3 Use the information you have gathered to make an illustrated guidebook for Christian pilgrims visiting this church.

Activity C

Imagine you are a British Jew, Christian or Muslim who has just returned from a pilgrimage to the Holy Land. You have been asked to write an article about your experiences for a magazine distributed in your religious community.

1 Start the article by explaining the preparations you made for your pilgrimage.
2 Describe where you went and what you did.
3 Include details about the history of the sites you visited and the beliefs people have about them.
4 Focus on the effect that your pilgrimage has had on you and how it may influence you in the future.

Activity D

It has been suggested that Jerusalem should be an international city, administered by the United Nations and not any single nation. This is because of its importance to the people of three religions.

1 Conduct some research into the history of the administration of Jerusalem.
2 Use the information you collect and your own judgement to write a letter to the Secretary General of the UN with your recommendations for the city. Should it be an international city?

Learning objectives

You will …
- find out about pilgrimage sites in India
- understand why India is important to different religions
- compare different views about pilgrimage.

The Indian subcontinent is the birthplace of three great religions: Hinduism, Buddhism and Sikhism. All of them have places associated with important events and beliefs. Visiting the sites can be a way for pilgrims to create positive **karma**.

Hinduism

Hindus call special places **tirthas**, which means river crossings. There are two reasons for this.

- Water is a precious commodity: nothing can live without it. As a result, many Hindu pilgrimage sites are rivers.
- Tirthas are spiritual crossings. They represent the meeting place of heaven and earth. They also symbolise movement through the cycle of birth, death and rebirth to reach **moksha**: freedom from the cycle.

Hinduism is a collection of different traditions, and each tradition has its own special places.

Varanasi

Varanasi is an ancient and mystical city on the banks of the River Ganges. For Hindus, the Ganges is the most holy of all rivers, and Varanasi is the most important centre of pilgrimage. Priests read from sacred texts and perform rituals. Pilgrims wash in the river, believing that the waters will wash away suffering and the effects of bad deeds. They reflect on the nature of life in the reality of death. Activity in the Ganges begins before dawn: as the sun rises on a new day, it brings hope for moksha.

Prayag

The rivers Ganges and Yamuna meet at Prayag. Pilgrims bathe in the rivers and make offerings for the dead. This is especially important at the times of the full moon and the new moon in the Hindu month of Magha. Once every twelve years the Kumbh Mela festival is held at Prayag. Hindu myths say that it will never be destroyed, even at the end of this universe.

Buddhism

Siddhartha Gautama, the Buddha, was born in a part of the Indian subcontinent that is today called Nepal. He spent most of his life travelling around northern India, teaching his followers about how to overcome suffering and be permanently happy. Many Buddhist pilgrimage sites are associated with events in the Buddha's life.

Lumbini

Lumbini is where Siddhartha was born. Today it is a peaceful place for pilgrims to meditate and reflect on the nature and meaning of life.

Bodh Gaya

When he was 35 years old, Siddhartha sat under a tree to meditate. He determined not to stop until he became **enlightened**. Today, a descendant of the original tree grows at the place where Siddhartha became a Buddha. The place is called Bodh Gaya. Pilgrims who visit will work to make progress towards their own enlightenment.

Sarnath

After becoming enlightened, the Buddha went to Sarnath and began to teach others how to become enlightened themselves. Buddhists visit the site today to reflect on the Buddha's teachings in the modern world.

Kusinara

The Buddha died at Kusinara. Buddhists believe that his enlightenment enabled him to pass away completely so that he would not be reborn. Pilgrims make offerings at temples and meditate on the impermanence of all things.

It was the Buddha himself who suggested that his followers should make pilgrimage to the four sites. He said they should 'visit and look upon (the places) with feelings of reverence'.

Sikhism

Unlike Hinduism, Sikhism teaches that pilgrimage is not a way to achieve moksha. Sikhs believe that, since God is everywhere and in everything, every place is special. They say that real pilgrimage is not a physical journey, but rather the search for God inside oneself. Nevertheless, many Sikhs choose to visit the Golden Temple at Amritsar. People from other faiths, and those of none, are also encouraged to visit it. It has four doors, one on each side, to show that it is accessible to all people, regardless of their background, sex or religion. In 1604 the completed **Adi Granth** was placed in the Temple. As the **Guru Granth Sahib**, it is the Sikhs' Guru for the rest of time. Its presence makes the Golden Temple the heart of the Sikh religion.

Knowledge check

1 What is a tirtha?
2 Which is the holiest of rivers for Hindus?
3 Which four pilgrimage sites are associated with the life of the Buddha?
4 What do the four doors of the Golden Temple symbolise?

Activity A

1 Find out more about the life of Siddhartha Gautama, particularly his birth, enlightenment, first sermon, and death.
2 Find an illustration of each event and insert each at the top of a new page in your workbook.
3 Underneath the illustrations, write the stories behind the events.

Activity B

1 Write an imaginary interview with a Sikh about pilgrimage and the Golden Temple.
2 You should create a dialogue in which the Sikh explains why pilgrimage is discouraged in Sikhism.
3 You should also provide an explanation about why the Golden Temple is important, even though it is not a place of pilgrimage.

Activity C

1 Why are rivers and lakes so important for Hindus as sacred sites? Find some examples to illustrate your answer.
2 Find out more about how water is used in Hinduism.
3 You could also find out about the importance of water in other religions.

Activity D

'There is no benefit to going on pilgrimage. It is all in the mind.'

1 What are the possible benefits of pilgrimage?
2 What reasons might someone have for saying that the benefits of pilgrimage are 'all in the mind'?
3 What is your view?

1.4 What makes a good leader?

Learning objectives

You will ...
- find out some qualities and characteristics that leaders have
- think of examples of good leaders
- analyse what good leadership means.

What is a leader?

A leader is someone who has followers. But what do good leaders have that make others want to follow?

In the Harry Potter books, Albus Dumbledore is the head of Hogwarts School. He believes in doing the right thing: 'It is our choices, Harry, that show what we truly are,' he says at one point. At another: 'It is important to fight, and fight again, and keep fighting, for only then can evil be kept at bay.'

Roy Hodgson is one of Britain's top football managers. What is his secret of success? 'The development of team spirit, developing pride in being a part of the team,' he says. Leaders need to motivate their teams: 'Use praise rather than a ticking-off. Show respect to people and players and build their confidence.'

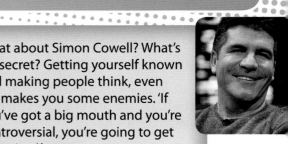

What about Simon Cowell? What's his secret? Getting yourself known and making people think, even if it makes you some enemies. 'If you've got a big mouth and you're controversial, you're going to get attention,' he says.

Steve Jobs, who led the Apple corporation, said that ideas and vision are what counts: 'If you are working on something exciting that you really care about, you don't have to be pushed. The vision pulls you.'

Jamie Oliver, TV chef, believes that passion is the key: 'When I do things that feel right, magic happens. I've done some amazing things, you know, and that's when I follow my heart. And when I never follow my heart I always get it wrong.'

So, here are five things that make a good leader.
- **An ability to motivate others**. Good leaders create trust in their followers and encourage them to work together. They make each person feel capable and strong.
- **A willingness to challenge**. Good leaders want to change things. Not everyone wants change, but good leaders will fight for their cause.
- **Passion for the cause**. Passion is infectious. Other people feel the passion of good leaders and share their enthusiasm.
- **Vision**. Good leaders want to make a difference, and they know how to go about it. They have a clear image of how things can change for the better.
- **Doing the right thing**. Good leaders have high standards. They know what is right, and will stop at nothing to achieve it.

Activity A

1 Think of a leader you know. It could be a teacher at school, the coach of a sports team, or even a friend.

2 Give examples of when they have demonstrated the five things that make a good leader.

Activity B

1 Find out about two or three major achievements of human beings in the history of the world.

2 Describe what the individuals concerned did to bring about the achievements and explain what qualities and characteristics they showed.

Knowledge check

1 What is a leader?

2 According to Jamie Oliver, what is the key to leadership success?

3 Who said, 'The vision pulls you?'

4 What are the five things that make a good leader?

Activity C

At the end of the 20th century, *Time* magazine asked its (mainly American) readers to vote for the most influential person of the century. Here, in order of popularity, are the top ten.

1 Elvis Presley
2 Yitzhak Rabin
3 Adolf Hitler
4 Billy Graham
5 Albert Einstein
6 Martin Luther King Jr.
7 Pope John Paul II
8 Gordon B. Hinckley
9 Mohandas (known as Mahatma) Gandhi
10 Ronald Reagan

1 Find out who each of these people was (all but one of them are dead now), and what they achieved.

2 Which of them were religious leaders, i.e. leaders of religious groups?

3 Which of those who did not lead religious groups had a strong religious faith?

4 For each religious leader, write a short paragraph about how their religious beliefs affected what they did in their lives.

5 Write up your findings as if you were writing an article for *Time*.

Activity D

Nelson Mandela was President of South Africa at the end of the last century, and considered by many to be a great leader. He said,

'Religion is one of the most important forces in the world. Whether you are a Christian, a Muslim, a Buddhist, a Jew, or a Hindu, religion is a great force, and it can help one have command of one's own morality, one's own behaviour, and one's own attitude.'

Do you agree that faith can help make people good leaders?

1.5 Who are religious leaders?

Learning objectives

You will ...
- learn words for different religious leaders
- understand why religious communities need to have leaders
- understand why some religious communities do not have leaders
- analyse the roles of religious leaders.

Nearly all groups and communities have leaders.
- Tutor groups have tutors.
- Sports teams have captains.
- Orchestras have conductors.
- Shops have managers.
- Cities have mayors.
- Films have directors.

The same is true of faith communities. The different religions have different titles for their leaders, and the functions of the leaders may differ. Even in the same religion, different groups give them different names and roles.

So, who are they?

Some religions distinguish between **ordained** and **lay** leaders.
- Someone who is ordained has been appointed to do a particular job in a religious community. They have usually received special training and are officially recognised in their role. It is likely to be their full-time occupation.
- Lay people are members of a faith community who are not professional religious leaders. Some may have leadership responsibilities, but they take these on as volunteers.

Buddhism

Ordained Buddhists are called **bhikkhus** (monks) or **bhikkhunis** (nuns). They have different roles in different Buddhist traditions. They live in monasteries and look after the spiritual needs of lay people in the local community. In return, the lay community supports them with food, clothing and money.

Christianity

Ordained leaders in different denominations have different titles and roles. In the Anglican, Catholic and Orthodox Churches, leaders who conduct services and look after lay people are called **priests**. Priests are looked after by **bishops**. In Protestant Churches, ordained leaders may be called **ministers** or **pastors**.

Judaism

The leader of a synagogue is a lay person, called the **president**. Ordained leaders are called **rabbis**. A rabbi is a teacher of the **Torah** and is trained to lead the Jewish community in their faith.

Sikhism

The Guru Granth Sahib is the teacher of Sikhs; there are no leaders and everyone is equal. **Gurdwaras** are managed by a committee of representatives, and the committee appoints a **granthi** who is responsible for looking after the Granth.

Hinduism

Traditionally, people born into the **Brahmin** caste were given the responsibility of keeping the sacred texts and performing religious rituals. Today, not all Brahmins are religious leaders. There are many types of people who are regarded as having religious authority, including gurus, yogis, swamis, pandits, acharyas, **sadhus** and rishis.

Islam

Community leaders are called **imams**. They lead prayers and give **sermons** in the mosque. There is no system of ordination in Islam. An imam is someone who is recognised as being knowledgeable about Islam and able to lead.

What do religious leaders do?

Religious leaders have responsibility for the care of their congregation or community.

They look after people's everyday needs, both practical and religious.

They lead rituals and services so that people can worship.

They try to stand out as examples of living correctly in their faith.

They try to help people who are troubled or are having difficulties with their faith.

They interpret religious teachings to make them relevant to their congregation.

They may try to attract new members to their congregation.

Some religious leaders can be recognised by what they wear.

Activity A

1 Choose one of the religious leaders you have read about in this chapter.

2 Write a job advertisement to recruit a leader for a particular religious community.

3 You should describe the duties the person will be expected to carry out and some of the personal qualities they will need to have.

Knowledge check

1 What are lay believers?

2 What is a bhikkhuni?

3 What are Muslim leaders called?

4 Who is in charge of a synagogue?

5 What does a granthi do?

Activity B

1 Read the text boxes in the section headed *What do religious leaders do?*

2 Rank them in order of importance. Mark the one that you think is most important 1, and so on down to 6.

3 Give reasons why you have chosen your order of importance.

Activity C

1 Find out more about the titles of religious leaders and what the titles mean.

2 What do the different names tell you about the roles of religious leaders?

3 Which leadership qualities do they need to show?

Activity D

1 Choose one of the religious leaders mentioned in this chapter.

2 Write a diary entry giving a typical day in that person's life.

3 What might the greatest problems and challenges be?

4 What might be the greatest rewards?

1.6 Can women be religious leaders?

Learning objectives

You will ...
- find out what religions teach about women in leadership roles
- understand why people have different opinions about women as religious leaders
- evaluate the fairness of religious teachings about women and leadership.

Do religions treat women unfairly?

A recent survey of British adults found that 40 per cent of women believed in God, whereas only 35 per cent of men did; 28 per cent of women did not believe in God, as opposed to 38 per cent of men.

It would seem that women, generally, are more religious than men.

And yet, in most religions, when it comes to leadership roles women seem to take second place to men. An article in the *New Statesman* said, 'A woman might one day become President of the United States; it seems highly unlikely that a woman will ever become Pope.'

Are religions sexist?

Some people think so. They say:
- Women aren't allowed to have leadership roles in the Catholic and Orthodox Churches.
- Muhammad and his successors were all men.
- The **Talmud** says that there are 48 male prophets in Judaism, but only seven female prophets.
- Religions refer to God as 'he'.
- Although women can become granthis, there are none in the UK.
- All of Jesus' disciples were men.
- It is more difficult for Buddhist women to be ordained than Buddhist men.
- Most Muslim communities will only allow men to be imams.
- Buddhist nuns have more rules to obey than Buddhist monks.
- Women are not allowed to become rabbis in Orthodox Judaism.
- In Hinduism, **puja** is usually led by men.

Other people disagree. They say:

- Women can and do have leadership roles in the Anglican and Protestant Churches.
- Women can be rabbis in Progressive Judaism.
- The Sikh scriptures say that women and men are equal.
- Jesus' mother, Mary, is an important figure in Catholic, Anglican and Orthodox Christianity, and is known as the Mother of God.
- Religions teach that God has no gender: 'he' is neither male nor female.
- Leadership roles are open to the women of many faiths, but they choose not to take them up.
- In many cases, it is culture and not religion that prevents women from taking on leadership roles.
- In all religions where only men can be leaders, there are groups of women fighting to change the situation.

Knowledge check

1 What percentage of women in the UK believe in God, according to a recent survey?

2 Which Christian denominations do not allow women to have leadership roles?

3 How many female granthis are there in the UK?

4 In which branch of Judaism can women become rabbis?

5 What do some Christians call Jesus' mother?

Activity A

1 Do you think that all religions are unfair to women when it comes to considering them for leadership positions?

2 Write a speech on the subject, giving reasons for your opinion.

Activity B

1 Write an imaginary interview with a member of one of the major religions.

2 Ask the interviewee questions suggesting that their religious organisation treats women unequally, using examples.

3 Write responses from the interviewee giving reasons why they believe that women are treated fairly in their religion.

Activity C

Employment, equality and sex discrimination laws in the UK make it against the law to stop women having the same job opportunities as men. However, organised religions are exempt from this law.

Do you think religions should be subject to the same laws as any other organisation? Give reasons and examples to support your point of view.

Activity D

In the Christian Bible, St Paul says,

'A woman should learn in quietness and full submission. I do not permit a woman to teach or to have authority over a man; she must be silent.'

(1 Timothy 2:12,13)

1 Should an instruction made nearly two thousand years ago apply today?

2 Write a report giving evidence to support your viewpoint.

1.7 How have religious leaders influenced the world?

Learning objectives

You will …
- find out about the achievements of some religious leaders
- understand the beliefs and values that inspired these leaders
- make links between people's beliefs and actions.

Since 1901, the Nobel Peace Prize has been awarded to the person who has 'done the most or the best work for fraternity between nations, the abolition or reduction of standing armies and for the holding and promotion of peace congresses.' It is one of the most prestigious awards a person can receive.

Many Nobel laureates (as recipients are called) have religious backgrounds. Some of them are religious leaders. Here are three.

The 14th Dalai Lama, 1989

The Dalai Lama is a Buddhist monk and teacher (**lama**). He became the religious and political leader of the people of Tibet in 1950, following the invasion of his country by the Chinese in 1949. He was sixteen years old. He tried to talk to Chinese leaders about their occupation of his country, but without success. By the end of the 1950s, it became clear that his life was in danger, so the Dalai Lama, along with his family and staff, secretly left Tibet. They travelled over the Himalayan mountains to India, where they were welcomed as guests of the Indian government.

The Dalai Lama was awarded the Nobel Peace Prize in 1989 in recognition of his non-violent campaign over nearly 40 years to end China's domination of his homeland.

In his acceptance speech on 10 December 1989, the Dalai Lama said, 'I believe the prize is a recognition of the true values of **altruism**, love, **compassion** and non-violence which I try to practise, in accordance with the teachings of the Buddha.'

He went on to say, 'As a Buddhist monk, my concern extends to all members of the human family and, indeed, to all **sentient** beings who suffer. I believe all suffering is caused by ignorance. People inflict pain on others in the selfish pursuit of their happiness or satisfaction. Yet true happiness comes from a sense of inner peace and contentment, which in turn must be achieved through the cultivation of altruism, of love and compassion and elimination of ignorance, selfishness and greed.'

Desmond Mpilo Tutu, 1984

Desmond Tutu began his career as a teacher in South Africa and then trained for the Anglican priesthood. At this time, South Africa, a country whose population is mainly black, was ruled by white people. Black people had to live apart from white people under a system called **apartheid**. As a black man, Tutu believed that this was wrong and became an outspoken critic of the white government. He became a bishop in 1976, and was awarded the Nobel Peace Prize in 1984 for 'his role as a unifying leader figure in the campaign to resolve the problem of apartheid in South Africa.'

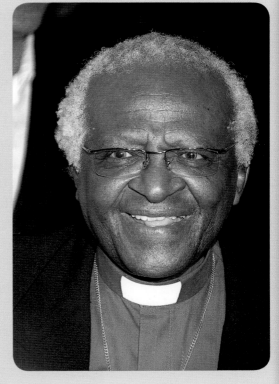

Apartheid in South Africa ended in 1991. In 1995, Desmond Tutu was asked to lead the Truth and Reconciliation Commission. His task was to collect evidence of human rights violations during the apartheid era, and recommend whether people who confessed to crimes should be pardoned. Since then, Tutu has been asked by other governments to advise them on setting up similar commissions.

In his Nobel lecture on 11 December 1984, Desmond Tutu said: 'When will we learn that human beings are of infinite value because they have been created in the image of God, and that it is a blasphemy to treat them as if they were less than this …? We can be human only in fellowship, in community … in peace. Let us work to be peacemakers … God calls us to be fellow workers with him, so that we can extend his Kingdom of **shalom**, of justice, of goodness, of compassion, of caring, of sharing, of laughter, joy and reconciliation, so that the kingdoms of this world will become the Kingdom of our God and of his Christ, and he shall reign forever and ever.'

Martin Luther King, Jr, 1964

Martin Luther King was born in Georgia, USA, in 1929, the son of a pastor in the Baptist Church. He followed in his father's footsteps and became pastor of a church in Montgomery, Alabama, in 1954. At that time, black people and white people in some states of America were **segregated** (separated). Facilities for white people were far better than those for blacks. Local laws emphasised the superiority of white people. For example, in Montgomery, black people had to sit behind white people on buses, and stand up so white people could sit down if a bus was full. As a black community leader, Martin Luther King successfully led a campaign against segregation on the buses. He went on to lead many more non-violent campaigns against injustice.

King was awarded the Nobel Peace Prize in 1964 for his work to end racial segregation through non-violent means. He was assassinated in 1968.

In his Nobel lecture on 11 December 1964, King said: 'This call for a worldwide fellowship that lifts neighbourly concern beyond one's tribe, race, class and nation is in reality a call for an all-embracing and unconditional love for all men … When I speak of love I am not speaking of some sentimental and weak response … I am speaking of that force which all of the great religions have seen as the supreme unifying principle of life. Love is somehow the key that unlocks the door which leads to ultimate reality.'

Knowledge check

1 When was the Nobel Peace Prize first awarded?
2 Which people does the Dalai Lama lead?
3 To which country did the Dalai Lama flee?
4 What is apartheid?
5 Which commission did Desmond Tutu lead in South Africa?
6 In which US city did Martin Luther King lead a campaign against segregation on the buses?
7 By what means did Martin Luther King work to end racial segregation?

Activity A

1 Here are some of the words that the Nobel laureates from this chapter used to describe their values (what is important to them):

compassion　　LOVE　　community

fellowship

2 See if you can find other positive values in the quotations on pages 24–26.

3 Use these words, and others you can think of, to describe what peace is.

4 Make a poster that illustrates these values, using photographs, symbols and colours.

Activity B

1 Find out about other religious Nobel laureates and nominees (people whose names were put forward for the prize but did not win it).

2 Make a presentation about their lives, their beliefs and their achievements.

Activity C

1 Use the Internet to find some quotations from one of the Nobel laureates featured in this chapter about their beliefs and values.

2 Explain what each quotation means, and try to find examples from that person's life of how they tried to put their beliefs into action.

3 You may also find photographs of your chosen person so that you can make a wall display.

Activity D

1 Imagine you have won the Nobel Peace Prize and have been asked to give a Nobel lecture.

2 Write a speech in which you explain what your idea of peace is and how it might be achieved.

3 You might find inspiration in some of the real Nobel laureates' lectures and acceptance speeches.

1.8 Why do some people live in religious communities?

Learning objectives

You will …
- learn what a mendicant is, and about mendicants in different religious traditions
- understand why some religious people live apart from society
- understand why some religions disapprove of mendicants.

For thousands of years, some religious people have chosen to live apart from society and devote their lives to the practice of their religion. This means they don't have families, jobs, homes, money or anything that will distract them from living their faith.

Such people are called **mendicants**. A mendicant is, literally, a beggar. A religious mendicant relies on people giving him or her food and clothes in order to survive.

Hindu mendicants are called sadhus. A sadhu is someone who leaves behind their life of possessions and comfort in order to concentrate on gaining moksha – freedom from the cycle of birth, death and rebirth. The word sadhu means one who aims to reach their goal.

In countries like India, sadhus are highly respected and inspire householders in their own faith. Therefore, householders are happy to give sadhus food. For sadhus, begging teaches them humility and gratitude.

Sadhus leave everyday life behind.

So they don't get distracted from their goal, sadhus will:
- own nothing, except their clothes and something to eat and drink from
- not have personal relationships, and will not have anything to do with women
- only eat and drink to stay alive
- not touch money.

Buddhist mendicants are called bhikkhus. A community of bhikkhus is called a **sangha**. The sangha was originally set up by the Buddha. Bhikkhus wander the countryside like sadhus, teaching people how to overcome life's sufferings to become permanently happy. During the rainy season – a period of about three months – the bhikkhus live together in a **vihara**.

Bhikkhus 'beg' for food every morning.

People who live near a vihara consider themselves fortunate, because they are able to contribute to its upkeep and provide food and robes for the bhikkhus. This means they can gain good karma.

Bhikkhus keep the same guidelines for living as sadhus. In addition, they have over 200 rules to keep so that they can live together peacefully.

Christians who wish to devote their lives to practising their faith away from the world are called **monks** if they are men or **nuns** if they are women. Traditionally, they live and practise alone but come together into communities so that they can support and learn from each other. They live simple lives in **monasteries** and try to be self-sufficient. Most Catholic and Anglican monks and nuns make promises of:

Christian monks pray for the world.

- obedience – to the Church
- poverty – giving up their possessions
- chastity – giving up relationships with the opposite sex.

Eastern Orthodox monks and nuns do not promise to follow rules. Their aim is to achieve eternal life with God by praying for the world. There are very few Protestant monasteries.

By and large, Muslims, Jews and Sikhs do not live as monks or nuns. They believe that they cannot serve and worship God by cutting themselves off from the world.

Sadhu means 'one who aims to reach a goal'.

Bhikkhu means 'one who wants to share'.

Monk means 'one who is solitary'.

Although Buddhist and Christian monks and nuns live in communities, their aim is for individual spiritual enlightenment. Hindu sadhus tend not to form communities.

Knowledge check

1 What is moksha?

2 Why do sadhus give up their ordinary lives?

3 What is the sangha?

4 Why do lay Buddhists give food and robes to bhikkhus?

5 What promises do many Christian monks and nuns make?

6 Why do Muslims, Jews and Sikhs generally not live as monks and nuns?

7 What does the word 'monk' mean literally?

Activity A

1 Draw up a chart comparing the lives of a sadhu, a bhikkhu and a Christian monk. You could refer to the meanings of their titles, the clothes they wear, how basic needs are provided, the rules they follow and their lifestyle.

2 Write a conclusion outlining what is similar and what is different.

Activity B

1 Write an FAQ page for the website of a Catholic or Orthodox monastery.

2 Think of things that people might want to know about monks and nuns, how they live, and what their goals are.

3 You may need to do some research to help you with the answers.

Activity C

1 Write an imaginary interview with a British bhikkhu living in a vihara in Britain.

2 Ask and answer questions about their beliefs and practices.

3 Ask and answer questions about how their beliefs and practices fit in with British culture and how they are accepted by British people.

4 Look at the websites of some British viharas to help you.

Activity D

'You can't achieve anything if you cut yourself off from the world.'

1 Why might most Muslims, Jews and Sikhs agree with this statement, and some disagree?

2 Why would Hindus, Buddhists and Christians disagree, and some agree?

3 What is your view?

The big assignment

Objectives

- To find out about sites of pilgrimages for a range of religions across the world.
- To understand the importance of the sites for religious people.
- To understand the effects that visiting pilgrimage sites may have on believers.

Outcome

You will produce a paper or electronic brochure describing a range of pilgrimage sites, and activities and practices that are associated with them, and explaining the religious importance of the sites.

Guidance

1   Work in groups of six. Each member of the group should specialise in a different religious tradition.

2   Each person in the group should research a range of pilgrimage sites from their specialist faith.

3   For each site, find out:

- for which religion or religions it is special
- what is there
- why it is there
- its history
- any symbolism associated with it
- what it is used for
- what pilgrims do when they visit it
- what special rules are associated with visiting it
- why it is important
- the effects that visiting it may have on pilgrims.

4   The specialist in Sikhism will need to explain Sikh teachings about pilgrimage and why some Sikhs still visit sites associated with events in the history of their faith.

5   Build up a collection of photographs of the sites you have researched.

6   Put together your photographs and research outcomes as either:

   a   hard-copy pages, or
   b   electronic pages.

7   Assemble the pages from all group members to create a brochure.

Assessment

You will be assessed on:

✓ how you use specialist vocabulary

✓ how you describe the pilgrimage sites

✓ how you explain the importance of the sites for pilgrims.

The following are all things that people may claim to know. But do they really? It all comes down to *how* they know. Where does their knowledge come from? And how reliable is it?

It's going to be sunny this weekend.

It rained last Tuesday.

The sum of 2 and 3 is 5.

My mum loves me.

Liam wouldn't lend me £5.

God loves me.

Sam's really mean.

Two times π is 6.2857.

Tia says she's not upset, but she is really.

I'm really upset, but I won't let it show.

Reason

Some things we know because we can work them out. We know 36 + 56 = 92 without using our senses. We know that black cats are black without having to see one. We use our power of reasoning.

The trouble is, simply working something out doesn't mean that we know it. We can reason that green cats are green, but that doesn't mean that there are any green cats.

Intuition

Sometimes people say they know something because they have a really strong feeling that it's true. You may think someone is lying to you, even though you can't explain why. You may be right.

On the other hand, you may be wrong.

Authority

We can claim to know things because we have them on good authority. If you want to find out the meaning of a word, you can look it up in a dictionary. You then know what the word means because you have used a trustworthy source.

However, authorities sometimes get things wrong, or different authorities may disagree with each other. Your doctor may tell you that you have appendicitis, when you actually have a stomach virus.

KNOWLEDGE

Revelation

Some people claim to know things that were revealed to them, perhaps in a vision or as a voice. For example, a person may dream which horse is going to win a race. They may be right. They may correctly predict the winners of ten races in a row based on their dreams.

Most people would say that, even if a dream turns out to be accurate, it could be coincidence or a lucky break.

Experience

We know about things around us through our senses. We can see, smell, feel, taste and hear the world around us, so we know that things exist and what they are like.

But experience is not completely reliable. Sometimes we think we see things that aren't there. Sometimes we mishear what people say.

Faith

You may have a great deal of confidence in someone or something. Your faith may lead you to say that you have knowledge. For example, you may lend a person some money and say that you know they will pay it back. You say this because you trust them. You may have good reason to trust them, because they have repaid you when you have lent them money before.

But, even if your faith is justified based on past experience, you may be let down.

Knowledge check

1 What do we call knowledge that comes through our senses?

2 What is reason?

3 What is intuition?

4 What is revelation?

Activity A

1 Make a chart to show the six sources of knowledge on page 35.

2 For each one, include an example that is true, and one that is false.

Activity B

1 Who do you have faith in? Make a list of those you trust most and, for each one, try to explain why.

2 Write about an example of when your faith in someone was rewarded.

3 Write about an example of when you were let down by someone you trusted.

4 Why is it important to have faith in people?

Activity C

1 Put the six sources of knowledge on page 35 into order, with the one you consider to be the most reliable at the top, and the least reliable at the bottom.

2 Give reasons for your rank order and examples.

Activity D

'The things you believe are more important than the things you know.'

1 What reasons might people have for agreeing with this statement?

2 Why might others disagree?

3 What do you think?

2.2 Does God exist?

Learning objectives

You will ...
- find out about some arguments for the existence of God
- compare the arguments
- understand why some people disagree with the arguments.

For most religious people, belief in God is central to their faith. If God does not exist, then their religion is meaningless. Often they claim to have knowledge of God and evidence for his existence.

Here are some of the arguments people have used to try to 'prove' that God exists, or at least that people should believe in him.

The Ontological Argument

(**Ontological** means 'to do with existence'.)

- What do people mean by 'God'? They mean God is a being that is so great that no greater being can be imagined.
- A thing that exists is greater than a thing that doesn't exist.
- If God doesn't exist, then things that do exist must be greater than him.
- But there can be nothing greater than God.
- Therefore, God must exist.

The Argument from Experience

- Some people have experiences of a spiritual nature that are so meaningful, even life-changing, that they cannot be explained scientifically.
- These experiences can't have come out of the blue. Someone or something must have made them happen.
- That someone or something is God.
- Therefore, God exists.

The Cosmological Argument

(**Cosmological** means 'to do with the universe'.)

- Everything is caused by something else.
- So the universe must have been caused by something.
- Whatever caused the universe is called God.
- Therefore, God exists.

Pascal's Wager

(Blaise Pascal was a French mathematician and philosopher.)

- If you believe in the God of Christianity, then, if he exists, you will receive a great reward in heaven.
- If you don't believe in the God of Christianity, then, if he exists, you will receive great punishment in hell.
- If you believe in the God of Christianity, then, if he doesn't exist, you will lose nothing.
- On balance, the outcomes of believing in God are much better than those of not believing in him. You have nothing to lose, after all.
- Therefore, you should believe in God.

The Argument from Utility

(**Utility** means 'usefulness'.)

- People have done and do great things because of their belief in God.
- They wouldn't have done these things if they didn't believe in God.
- Therefore, it doesn't matter whether God does or doesn't exist. Believing in him is the most important thing.

The Argument from Miracles

- Sometimes, things happen that seem to go against the laws of nature. For example, people are cured of illnesses that are incurable.
- The laws of nature can only be broken by someone or something that is **supernatural** (i.e. above the laws of nature).
- That someone or something is God.
- Therefore, God exists.

The Argument from Morality

- Morals are rules that tell us how to behave. For example, *It is wrong to kill* means that you shouldn't kill; *It is good to tell the truth* means that you should tell the truth.
- There must be someone or something that made up the rules.
- That someone or something is God.
- Therefore, God exists.

The Argument from Design

- There is order in the universe. It is like a big machine, everything in it working together.
- The way everything works together is evidence that the universe has design and purpose.
- If something is designed, then there must be a designer.
- That designer is God.
- Therefore, there must be a God.

Some people say that the arrangement of the universe is proof that God exists.

Knowledge check

1 What does ontological mean?
2 What word means 'to do with the universe'?
3 Which argument says believing in God is more important than his existence?
4 Which argument says that God tells us how to behave?
5 Who was Blaise Pascal?

Activity A

1 Which of the arguments do you think is the best?
2 Which of the arguments is the least convincing?
3 What is your view about the existence of God?
4 Give reasons for your view.

Activity B

1 Choose one of the arguments for the existence of God.
2 What reasons might someone have for disagreeing with it?
3 Write a script of an imaginary discussion between someone arguing for the existence of God and someone arguing against it.

Activity C

1 Put the arguments for the existence of God on pages 37–38 in rank order, the most convincing at the top.
2 Produce a PowerPoint® presentation on attempted proofs of God's existence.
3 For each argument, present as many counter-arguments as you can. Some research on the Internet will help you find some.

Activity D

1 Match the arguments for the existence of God with the sources of knowledge from Chapter 2.1.
2 Write a report entitled *Can we ever know that God exists*?

2.3 Where do our ideas come from?

Learning objectives

You will …
- learn what socialisation is
- find out about the agents of socialisation
- know what people learn from the agents of socialisation
- understand how people learn from the agents of socialisation.

Imagine …

You're walking home from school one day when everything around you becomes covered in shadow. You look up and the sky is hidden by an expanse of metal. It is the underside of an alien space craft. Before you have time to react, a tube descends from the ship, and you are sucked inside …

The same tube that sucked you into the space craft spits you out into a place you have never been before. Nothing you see and hear is familiar to you …

It's a bit like being born. A baby enters a world that is completely strange to it. It has to learn to fit in, to be part of its community. And a baby born in a city in Britain will have to learn different things from one born in a remote village in Namibia, for example.

What have you had to learn in order to survive? And where did you learn from?

You need to know different things to survive in different settings.

The process of learning to fit into society is called **socialisation**.

School
School not only teaches you the knowledge and skills you need to pass exams. You also learn things like punctuality and how to be smart to help you in later life.

Peers
Your peers are people of your own age. You learn what you have to be like and what you have to do to make relationships.

Media
The **media** include TV and radio, the Internet, magazines and newspapers, music and music videos, and adverts. We are surrounded by the media. The media teach us about our culture.

SOCIALISATION

Religion
Religion teaches values and morals, and helps us think about important questions of life and death. The importance of religion for socialisation varies among families and societies.

Family
Your family introduces you to the things that are expected of you in society. You learn how to talk, how to walk, the basic rules of hygiene. Children pick up on their parents' beliefs, attitudes and values. They learn what adults should be like.

A recent survey found that children in the UK spend an average of 4.5 hours a day watching TV or online. Over a year, that's more time than they spend in lessons at school.

The institutions that socialise us are called **agents of socialisation**.

Knowledge check

1 What is socialisation?
2 What is an agent of socialisation?
3 What are the agents of socialisation?
4 From which agent or agents do people learn how to make relationships?
5 How much time do children in the UK spend watching TV or online, on average?

Activity A

1 Make a poster for new pupils at your school that tells them about how to make friends and get on with people.
2 You should include rules about how to get on with adults as well as peers.

Activity B

1 Conduct a survey among pupils and adults at your school to find out the most important things a child can be taught.
2 Present your findings in a chart.
3 Write an explanation of what your chart shows.

Activity C

1 Make a PowerPoint® presentation about the agents of socialisation.
2 For each agent, list as many things as you can that it teaches people.
3 Write a conclusion to explain which of the agents of socialisation you think is most important, and why.

Activity D

1 Write an essay on how the media portray religion and religious people.
2 Try to find examples of both positive and negative portrayals.
3 Use examples from as many different media as you can.
4 In your conclusion, say whether, in general, religion is represented in a favourable light or not.

2.4 Why do people say God exists?

Learning objectives

You will …
- find out how religion has developed over time
- understand why some people accept belief in God and other religious beliefs
- analyse people's reasons for holding religious beliefs.

People have had religious beliefs for as long as they have lived in the world.

A very brief history of religious beliefs

- Primitive societies had **gods** to represent **forces of nature**. They would **pray** to them for help in **growing crops** or **hunting**.
- Later, people would ask their gods to **protect them against their enemies**.
- In the first cities, people had local gods. **Worshipping** together helped to keep **communities** close.
- **State leaders** became gods, and people had to worship them. In this way, rulers could **keep control** over their people.
- Some people challenged bad rulers by saying that the gods were **displeased** with them and would take their **power** away.
- People started to think of **religion** as a way to help them to a better **life after death**.
- People used their religious beliefs to make **moral rules** so that people would lead **good lives**.

Today, religious people cover the planet. There is not a single society that does not have religion. It is estimated that about 85 per cent of the world's population is religious.

People have all sorts of reasons for believing in God or turning to religion. These are some of the things they say.

My family is religious. I was brought up that way.

I got to know some people who were religious, and they really impressed me.

When my mum was ill, I prayed and she got better.

This is a Christian country, so I am a Christian.

My faith is my business. It works for me, whatever anyone else says.

I can't believe that the universe happened by chance.

People have all sorts of reasons for believing ...

I can't explain why I believe in God. I just know he's there.

I wasn't brought up to be religious, but life without faith just seemed rather shallow.

I became a Catholic because my wife is a Catholic.

When I had surgery at hospital, I had a sort of dream, like a vision of heaven.

My family is religious. They would be really upset if I wasn't.

Some people came to my house. What they told me about their faith really made sense to me.

As I've got older, I think more about life and death and I've started to think there must be a God.

Knowledge check

1 What did the gods of primitive societies represent?

2 What effect did worship have in the first cities?

3 What percentage of the world's population is thought to be religious?

Activity A

1 Write out the beginnings of thirteen statements as follows, 'Some people are religious because …'

2 Use the quotations on page 44 to help you finish the statements, so that you end up with a list of reasons why people are religious. See how many you can come up with.

3 Which of your statements gives the best reason for believing in God or being religious?

4 Give reasons why you think this is the best reason.

Activity B

1 Complete parts 1 and 2 of Activity A.

2 Put the statements into rank order, with the one that gives the best reason for believing in God or being religious at the top.

3 Explain why you have put them in this order.

4 Try to match each statement with one of the sources of knowledge, arguments for the existence of God or agents of socialisation from the previous three chapters of this book.

Activity C

1 The French writer, Voltaire, said, 'If God did not exist, it would be necessary to invent him.'

2 What evidence is there in the history of religion to back up Voltaire's view?

Activity D

1 Every society has religious or supernatural beliefs. Is this proof that religion is true, or that human beings are somehow programmed to be religious?

2 Try to present both sides of the argument.

2.5 Why are people religious?

Learning objectives

You will ...
- understand why people are religious
- analyse some of the reasons people have for being religious
- be able to link people's religious beliefs with the effects they have on their lives.

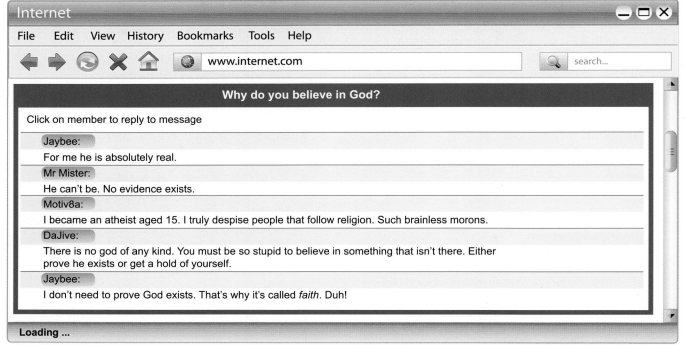

Internet

File   Edit   View   History   Bookmarks   Tools   Help

www.internet.com   search...

Why do you believe in God?

Click on member to reply to message

Jaybee:
For me he is absolutely real.

Mr Mister:
He can't be. No evidence exists.

Motiv8a:
I became an atheist aged 15. I truly despise people that follow religion. Such brainless morons.

DaJive:
There is no god of any kind. You must be so stupid to believe in something that isn't there. Either prove he exists or get a hold of yourself.

Jaybee:
I don't need to prove God exists. That's why it's called *faith*. Duh!

Loading ...

(From an online message board)

It seems that proving the existence of God may be more important for some **atheists** than **theists**.

This is how one Christian put it:

> 'Faith in God is a gift from God. You can pray and ask for the faith to know and follow him. Then you can receive God's guidance in your life and get to heaven after you die. Knowing God can transform your life. When you know God, and pray about your life, God can help you live a better life. As God is love, life is primarily about love and making relationships in order to have a rich and full life.'

For this person, the importance of faith is the effect that it has on his or her life. What other reasons do people have for following their faith?

My belief gives me strength to carry on in my everyday life. I believe religion empowers you spiritually. It takes you to a place you didn't know you had.

I believe in God because I was in a very sad place. I practised the teachings, and that's given me the courage to face each day. Most of the stuff is common sense.

I sort of see the presence of God in everything that is alive (including myself). So part of my faith gives me the feeling of being connected with the greater web of life. I get the fulfilment of knowing that I am part of something much larger and greater than myself.

I get peace of mind, happiness and a way to live, and attempt to make the world a better place.

I don't believe God can make vast improvements in my life, but he certainly can provide me with more than enough motivation and strength to do that myself.

Religion gives me purpose in this life and a desire to choose the right path.

Islam gives me self-respect, knowledge and patience, and also a great reward in the afterlife, **Insha'Allah**.

If I didn't believe in God I would find life very pointless. You live, you work, you go through all sorts of pain and in the end you just go back to so many carbon molecules in the ground? It doesn't sit right with me. And although I'm not the person I'd like to be, believing in God gives me hope that eventually I'll end up being a better person, and it will all be worth it.

Knowledge check

1 Which word is used to mean someone who believes there is no God?

2 What is a theist?

3 List three things from the quotations on page 47 that people believe God gives them.

Activity A

1 Continue the conversation on the message board on page 46.

2 Remember that in the course of the messaging conversation, some participants should give reasons why they practise a religion.

3 Others should explain why they do not.

Activity B

1 Write an essay entitled, 'Why are people religious?'

2 Use the quotations on page 47 to give as many reasons as you can.

Activity C

1 Write a booklet called *Life: a self-help guide*.

2 It should contain ideas about how to lead a fulfilling life.

3 Include both religious and non-religious ideas.

Activity D

'If I didn't believe in God I would find life very pointless.'

1 Explain what this quotation means.

2 In your explanation, use some of the other ideas contained in this chapter.

3 Do you agree that people need a purpose to their lives?

4 Why might someone disagree with you about this?

2.6 Are we free to choose?

Learning objectives

You will …
- understand why some people may say that their lives are planned in advance
- analyse the idea of free will
- find out what the major religions teach about free will.

Religious people have a bit of a problem.
- The Cosmological argument says that everything has a cause, and that nothing happens by chance.
- The Argument from Design says that God designed the universe, so everything happens because God wants it to.
- Religious people say that there is a purpose to life.
- Some religious people say that God has a plan for everyone.

So, here's the problem. If all this is true, then human beings aren't free to make their own decisions. Their lives are all planned in advance.

Modern science seems to back this up.
- Experts can predict accurately events that will happen in the future. Eclipses, tides and the times the sun will rise and set are predictable for thousands of years into the future.
- What a person looks like is determined by genes passed from their parents – and their genes may determine whether or not they are likely to get serious diseases later in life.
- There are laws that make people behave as they do. Genetics, agents of socialisation, psychological makeup: these things affect the ways people act.
- Even things that can't be predicted at the moment may be foreseeable in the future.

Muslims believe in **predestination**. This is a belief that, because God is in complete control of the universe, he knows in advance everything that will happen. He knows what decisions each person will make before they make them. Human beings still have free will, however. They are free to choose: it's just that God knows what choices they will make.

This child is free to choose the ice cream or the spinach. You know which one he will choose, don't you? But still the child has a free choice. Muslims say this is what predestination is like.

Hindus, Buddhists and Sikhs believe in **karma**: everything that happens to you is caused by something you have done before. So, although your life is decided in advance, it is you who do the deciding. And when something happens to you as a result of your karma, you have the freedom to choose how you deal with it: whether to create good or bad karma for the future.

Jews and Christians would say that when God created the universe, he created human beings to have free will: the power to make their own decisions and control their actions. So humans can choose whether to do good deeds or evil ones. They can even choose whether to believe in God or not. But they will eventually have to face the consequences of their decisions and actions.

Christianity teaches that God will forgive anyone who turns to him and is truly sorry for things they have done wrong.

Judaism teaches that if you hurt someone else, then, if you are truly sorry, God will help that person to forgive you.

Knowledge check

1 Which argument for the existence of God says that everything that happens has been caused by something else?

2 Which religion teaches that God will forgive anyone who turns to him and is sorry for what they have done wrong?

3 What does Judaism teach about forgiveness?

4 What is predestination?

5 Which religions teach about karma?

Activity A

1 Make a list of choices that are made for you by other people.

2 Make a list of things you would like to do, but can't do.

3 What and who prevent you from doing as you please?

4 Now write a paragraph to answer the question, 'Are you completely free to make your own decisions about your life?'

5 Give reasons and provide examples.

6 Write a concluding paragraph to explain whether or not you should be able to do anything you want.

Activity B

1 Draw up a chart comparing the teachings of the different religions on the subject of free will.

2 Your chart should show similarities and differences between them.

Activity C

1 How might a Muslim respond to someone who says, 'If everything is controlled by Allah, then I may as well do nothing. I'll just sit back and wait for things to happen.'?

2 How might a Hindu respond to someone who says, 'There is no point in helping poor people. If things are going to get better for them, they will, with or without me.'?

3 How might a Buddhist respond to someone who says, 'If someone is homeless, they have caused it to happen. My giving money won't do anything to change their karma.'?

4 How might a Christian respond to someone who says, 'If I see a beggar and don't help, it doesn't matter. God will forgive me anyway.'?

Activity D

1 Are people responsible for everything they do?

2 Are they responsible for everything that happens to them?

3 Refer to different religious teachings in your answer.

4 What is your view?

2.7 Why do people suffer?

51

Learning objectives

You will ...
- find out the differences between moral suffering and natural suffering
- understand why some people think that suffering in the world gives reasons to doubt the existence of God
- understand how religion tries to explain why God allows suffering
- be able to evaluate reasons to explain why God allows suffering.

Now religious people have another problem. People who believe in God say that he created the universe and human beings in it. They say that he loves the things he created. They also say that he is **omnipotent**. If this is what God is like, how can there be suffering in the world? How can God allow it?

Suffering from moral causes

A lot of suffering in the world is caused by human beings being bad. People do nasty things to each other, like theft, murder or racist abuse. Sometimes, governments can cause suffering when they torture their citizens or declare war on another country.

Many religious people would say that this kind of suffering is not God's fault. Human beings have free will, and some choose to be cruel. But why are innocent people victims of other people's cruelty? They do not deserve it.

Suffering from natural causes

Suffering is also caused by nature. Earthquakes, tsunamis, droughts and volcano eruptions just happen; people don't make them happen. But if God made the world, why did he make it that way? How do religious teachings explain natural suffering?

How can God allow people to suffer in his world?

'We are happy to suffer, because suffering makes us strong.'
(From the Christian Bible)

'We are suffering from our own sins.'
(From the Jewish Bible)

'Greed, anger and stupidity are like a fever. If a man gets a fever, even if he lies in a comfortable room, he cannot rest. In the same way, greed, anger and stupidity are the sources of all human suffering.'
(From the Buddhist scriptures)

'For any adversity a Muslim suffers, Allah erases some of his sins.'
(Hadith: a saying of Muhammad – Islam)

'Many good things would be taken away if God permitted no evil to exist.'
(Thomas Aquinas – Christian thinker)

'God would not allow any evil to exist unless out of it he could draw a greater good. This is part of the wisdom and goodness of God.'
(St Augustine – Christian thinker)

'We test you by evil and by good by way of trial.'
(From the Qur'an)

'Suffer what there is to suffer; enjoy what there is to enjoy. Regard both suffering and joy as facts of life.'
(Nichiren – Buddhist teacher)

'Christians remind me of schoolboys who want to look up the answers to their maths problems in the back of the book rather than work them through.'
(Søren Kierkegaard – Christian)

Buddhism doesn't have to explain how God can allow suffering, because Buddhists don't believe in a loving God. Buddhism teaches that suffering is a fact of life: it is just the way life is. The word Buddhists use is **dukkha**. Dukkha doesn't just mean suffering. To say that life is dukkha means that life is unsatisfactory. Things don't always go the way we want them to and we get disappointed. The only way to avoid being disappointed is not to want things in the first place.

Knowledge check

1 What does omnipotent mean?
2 Which question do religious teachings find it difficult to answer?
3 What is moral suffering?
4 What is natural suffering?
5 Which religion does not teach about a loving God?
6 What does dukkha mean?

Activity A

1 Write a letter to God giving the reasons why some people find it hard to believe in a loving God.
2 In your letter, include examples of undeserved suffering.
3 How might God respond to your letter?

Activity B

1 Use the quotations in this chapter to make a list of reasons religious people use to explain why there is suffering in the world.
2 For each one, give your opinion on how convincing it is as an explanation.
3 Do you think it is possible to believe in God when there is suffering in the world?

Activity C

1 Research Buddhist teachings about the Four Noble Truths and the Noble Eightfold Path.
2 How convincing do you think the Buddhist explanation for the cause of suffering is?
3 How convincing are Buddhist teachings about how to overcome suffering?

Activity D

1 Write a list of examples of natural suffering.
2 For each one, try to think of how human beings caused it, contributed to it or made it worse.
3 Now write a short dialogue between two people discussing the idea that human beings bring about their own suffering.

2.8 When are the beginning and end of life?

Learning objectives

You will ...
- find out about different views on what a person is
- find out about the stages of pregnancy
- understand why people have different views about when life starts and finishes
- think about what you believe about the beginning and end of life.

When does life begin and end?

This may seem a bit of a daft question. It seems obvious that life begins at birth and ends at death. It starts when there is a new person and finishes when that person ceases to exist.

This opens up a much bigger question:

What is a person?

There is no definite answer to this question. Different people have different views. Here are some of them.

A person is a being that is aware of its own existence, and is aware of its surroundings.

A person is a being that has free will.

A person is a being that is able to think.

A person is a being that has a soul.

A person is a being that can feel emotions.

A person is a being that can feel pain.

When does a person become a person?

It is clear that a newborn baby is a person. But when did it become a person? Here are the stages of development before a baby is born.

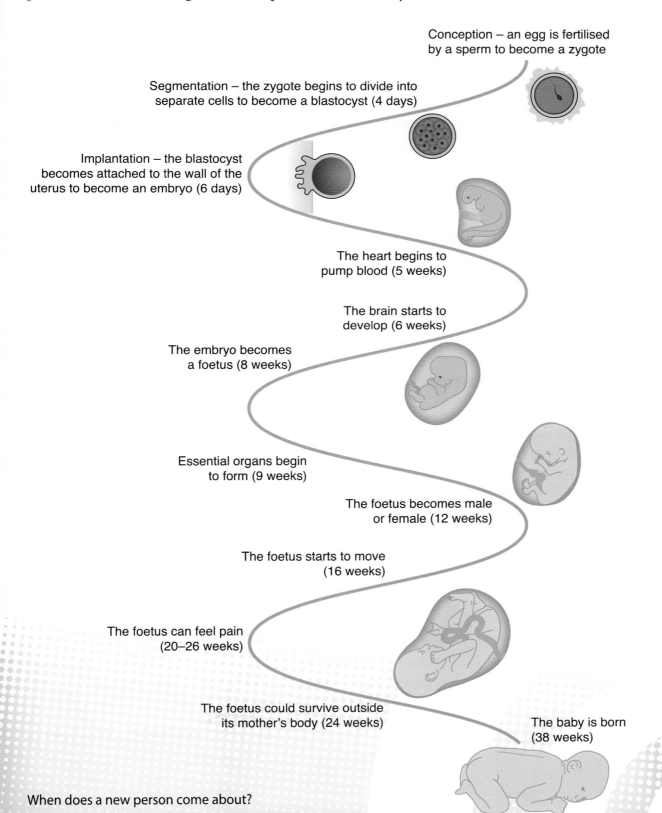

Conception – an egg is fertilised by a sperm to become a zygote

Segmentation – the zygote begins to divide into separate cells to become a blastocyst (4 days)

Implantation – the blastocyst becomes attached to the wall of the uterus to become an embryo (6 days)

The heart begins to pump blood (5 weeks)

The brain starts to develop (6 weeks)

The embryo becomes a foetus (8 weeks)

Essential organs begin to form (9 weeks)

The foetus becomes male or female (12 weeks)

The foetus starts to move (16 weeks)

The foetus can feel pain (20–26 weeks)

The foetus could survive outside its mother's body (24 weeks)

The baby is born (38 weeks)

When does a new person come about?

So when does the life of a person start? People have different views.

At conception

'All human life, from the moment of conception [the beginning of pregnancy] and through all subsequent stages ... is sacred, because human life is created in the image and likeness of God.'

(Pope John Paul II)

'Was he (a person) not a drop of sperm? Then he became a clot of blood and God shaped and formed and made of him a pair, the male and the female.'

(From the Qur'an)

When blood appears

'For the life of the flesh is in the blood.'

(From the Jewish and Christian Bibles)

When the foetus can survive outside its mother's body

'When does it have the moral status of a human being? When does it have some kind of awareness of its surroundings? When it can feel pain, for example, because that's one of the most brute kinds of awareness there could be. And that happens, interestingly enough, just around the time of viability. It certainly doesn't happen with an embryo.'

(Professor Bonnie Steinbock – philosopher)

When the baby is born

'Antoninus asked Rabbi Judah: "From when is the soul endowed in man: from the time of birth, or from the moment of intercourse?" Rabbi Judah answered, "From the time of birth."'

(From the **Talmud** – Judaism)

When does a person stop being a person?

This used to be a simple question to answer: a person is dead when their heart stops beating. But medical technology has made things complicated.

- It is possible to keep someone's heart beating and organs working on a life-support machine, even if the brain has stopped working. Is this a person?
- Doctors can turn off life-support machines when the brain is dead. One time in a thousand, the body continues to survive after the machine has been turned off, though the brain remains dead. Is this a person?
- It is possible to be in a vegetative state. This is when some sections of the brain are working, but there is no awareness of surroundings, no feelings of pain or pleasure, no understanding of speech, no thoughts, no emotions and no memories. Is this a person?

Knowledge check

1 What is a zygote?

2 At what stage of pregnancy does an embryo become a foetus?

3 About how long is human pregnancy?

4 At what stage of pregnancy does life start, according to the Roman Catholic Church?

5 According to the Talmud, when does a human being become a person?

6 What is a vegetative state?

Activity A

1 When do you think a human being becomes a person?

2 Try to give reasons for your view and show that you have thought about other views.

Activity B

1 Read the scenarios described under the heading, *When does a person stop being a person?*

2 Answer the questions at the end of them, and give reasons for your answers.

3 How would you define a person?

4 Take into account the different definitions in this chapter.

Activity C

1 Find out more religious and secular views about when life starts and about abortion.

2 Explain why people have different opinions about abortion.

Activity D

1 Why is it important to ask about when a human being becomes a person and what a person is?

2 Find out about different issues that are affected by views on what a person is, and when life starts and finishes.

3 Make a PowerPoint® presentation or wall display on some of these issues and the range of views about them.

The **big** assignment

Task

To make a documentary about believing in God.

Objectives

- To know why some people believe in God and why some people believe there is no God.

- To understand how believing in God affects people's lives.

- To be able to present arguments for and against the existence of God.

Outcome

A documentary film, or the script for a film, about why some people believe in God and why some people don't.

Guidance

1 Work in groups of four. Each member of the group should represent a different view or tradition:

- Christianity, Islam or Judaism
- Hinduism or Sikhism
- Buddhism
- atheism.

2 As a group, decide on a list of questions that explore why people believe or don't believe in God.

3 Your questions should be about:

- arguments for the existence of God
- socialisation and belief in God
- differences between believing and knowing
- how believing in God affects people's lives
- whether or not people have free will
- whether or not God has plans for individual people
- whether or not God has control of people's lives
- how to explain the existence of evil and suffering in the world.

4 Each member of the group should find out how a person of the view or tradition they represent would answer the questions, and then write a script in the form of an interview.

5 Either video the interviews, taking it in turns to be the interviewer, or put together a PowerPoint® presentation of the interview scripts.

Assessment

You will be assessed on:

✓ how you use specialist vocabulary

✓ how you explain views about believing in God

✓ how you explain how believing in God affects people's lives.

Is your life your own?

When people talk about their pets, they talk about them as if they own them. In a sense they do, especially if they bought them.

- Dog owners may keep their pets on a lead.
- Hamster owners may keep their pets in a cage.
- When pet owners move house, they take their animals with them, along with all the other things they own.

Maybe you feel like your life isn't your own sometimes.

- Your parents tell you what to do. If you disobey them, you get grounded.
- Your teachers tell you what not to do. If you disobey them, you get put in detention.

If you have a job, then someone is, quite literally, buying your time.

- The time you're being paid for is not your own any more.
- You have to do what you are paid to do.

All this means that you have responsibilities towards other people. But does it mean they own you?

Have you ever wondered why some Christian ministers wear a round collar (sometimes called a 'dog collar')? Some say it represents the big iron collar worn by slaves in the Roman Empire. It shows that they are 'slaves' to God and 'servants' to God's people.

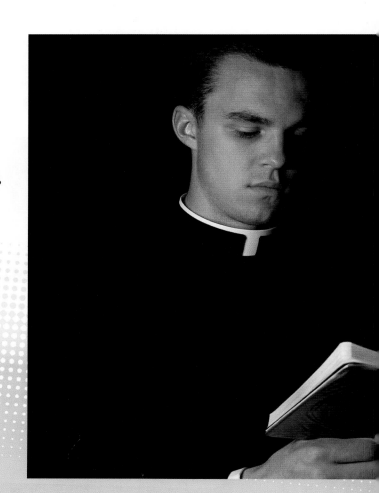

Many religious people would say that a person's life is not their own. It is given to them as a gift from God. As with any other gift, they are free to do what they want with it. But they still have a responsibility to God to treat it with care and respect. For religious people, life is the most precious gift a person can receive. For this reason, it is not up to them to decide when it should end.

'Before I formed you in the womb I knew you.'
(Jeremiah 1:5)

'The kingdom of God is within you.'
(Luke 17:21)

'God created man in his own image.'
(Genesis 1:27)

Why do Christians say that human life belongs to God?

'You, dear children, are from God.'
(1 John 4:4)

'For you created my inmost being … in my mother's womb.'
(Psalm 139:13)

Christians believe that human life is holy or sacred. This idea is known as the **sanctity of life**.

What do Buddhists believe about life?

Buddhism teaches that there is no such thing as a soul (**anatta**). This means that they don't believe in a self. For them, the whole idea of having an individual self is an illusion. Some Buddhists would say that life is like an ocean. If you take a drop of water from it, the drop appears to be separate from the rest of the ocean. But it is an illusion. If you put the drop back, you will never find it again.

Buddhists believe that lives are connected, rather like pieces in a jigsaw puzzle. Each piece does not show you the whole picture; yet the picture is not complete if one piece is missing.

For Buddhists, every life is special because it is connected to every other life.

So, Buddhists believe that your life is not yours, because there is no 'you': everything is connected. This is why they believe that by harming another being, you are causing harm to yourself (**karma**).

Knowledge check

1 What is the possible origin of the Christian minister's dog collar?
2 Who do Christians say life belongs to?
3 What does anatta mean?
4 Which religion teaches about anatta?
5 For Buddhists, how is a person's life like a drop of ocean water?

Activity A

1 Make a wall display to show how special human life is.
2 Include some photographs in the display that show how precious it is.
3 Write a paragraph to put beside your display explaining what it shows.

Activity B

1 Write an article to explain to atheists why life is special for Christians.
2 Use the ideas contained in the quotations in this chapter in your explanation.

Activity C

1 Make a chart to show what Christian and Buddhist attitudes might be towards:
   - abortion
   - euthanasia
   - suicide.
2 Try to show where people of the same religion may have different views.
3 Provide some reasons for the different views.

Activity D

How would you answer the question, 'Whose life is it?' You should refer to religious and secular ideas in your response.

3.2 Can war ever be justified?

Learning objectives

You will ...
- find out why some religious people believe war is sometimes necessary
- understand the conditions of the Just War
- find out what a martyr is
- understand why some people are prepared to give up their lives for their beliefs
- analyse the role of religion in war.

Religions teach that human life is infinitely precious. Yet, when people criticise religion, they often refer to the number of people who kill or are killed in the name of religion.

What about killing?

'We make war that we may live in peace.'

(Aristotle, an ancient Greek philosopher)

Some religious people agree with Aristotle.

Many Christians believe that sometimes going to war may be a better option than not going to war. This is known as the **Just War** theory. (Just means morally right.) For a country to declare a Just War, certain conditions have to be met.

- There must be a **good reason**.
- The war must be approved by a **recognised authority**, like the **United Nations**.
- It must be a **last resort**.
- It must aim to **make things better**.
- The **country** should have a **good chance of winning**.
- It should use no more force than is needed to **achieve its aims**.

Islam teaches that doing what God requires can be a struggle. The word Muslims use for struggle is **jihad**. If a Muslim nation feels it must go to war to defend Islam, the war may be called a military jihad.

Judaism teaches that war is sometimes necessary.
- This may be in self-defence.
- If the Jewish nation believes it is about to be attacked, it may strike first.
- War may be declared to protect Jewish interests.

Sikhism also teaches that war may be fought against cruelty or to protect the innocent.

In war, Muslims, Jews and Sikhs follow guidelines similar to the conditions of the Just War.

What about dying?

'If a man hasn't discovered something he will die for, he isn't fit to live.'
(Martin Luther King)

So, some religious people believe that it is sometimes necessary to kill for what is right. In the same way, some believe it may be necessary to die for what is right.

A person who dies for a cause they believe is right is called a **martyr**.

Maksymilian Kolbe was a Polish priest. During the Second World War he was imprisoned in a concentration camp for helping Jews escape capture by the Nazis. When three men escaped from the camp, ten prisoners were chosen at random to be starved to death. One of them cried out for his family, and Kolbe volunteered to take his place. In the starvation cell, Kolbe led prayers each day. He was the last to die.

In the first century CE, Jews fought against the Romans who occupied the land they believed had been promised to them by God. One group of Jews took themselves to a hilltop fortress called Masada. The Romans could not get to them until they built a ramp up to the top. When they finally entered the fortress, they discovered that the Jews had taken their own lives rather than face capture by their oppressors.

In 1757, the Afghan army raided Northern India. The Sikhs fought back and, in revenge, the Afghans destroyed the Sikhs' Golden Temple. Baba (Saint) Deep Singh led a group of Sikhs, first to rebuild the temple, and then to punish the Afghan leader and his army. The Sikhs won the battle, but Baba Deep Singh lost his life. His sword (which weighed 16 kilograms) is still preserved today, and Sikhs sprinkle rose petals on the spot where Baba Deep Singh fell as a mark of respect.

The death of a martyr can inspire the faith of religious people.

Knowledge check

1 What is a Just War?
2 What does jihad mean?
3 What is a military jihad?
4 What is a martyr?
5 What nationality was Maksymilian Kolbe?
6 Why did the Jews of Masada kill themselves?
7 Who was Baba Deep Singh fighting when he was killed?

Activity A

1 Find out more about martyrs from different religions.
2 Write out their stories, explaining what causes they were defending.
3 You could make a booklet of the stories you collect.

Activity B

1 Write an imaginary interview with a Christian, Muslim, Jew or Sikh who believes that war is sometimes necessary.
2 You should ask questions that would get them to explain how fighting and killing can be justified.

Activity C

1 Camilo Torres was a Christian priest in Colombia in South America. In his time, Colombia was ruled by a corrupt and cruel government and many people were extremely poor. Torres believed that the only way to help the poor was to join a guerrilla army and fight for justice. He was killed in combat.
2 Find out about Torres' life and beliefs, and make a presentation about them.
3 Torres once said, 'If Jesus were alive today, he would be a revolutionary fighter.' Explain why he believed this.
4 Do you agree with him? Give reasons for your answer.

Activity D

1 Do you agree that religion is a major cause of war?
2 Try to present different points of view, backed up by reasons.
3 You could find some examples of conflict to illustrate your account.

Learning objectives

You will ...
- find out about two pacifists from history
- understand what ahimsa means for Buddhists
- understand why Quakers are pacifists
- reflect on ways in which people can live together peacefully
- compare different views about war and peace.

Nobody likes the idea of war. Yet many people, including religious people, believe that it is sometimes better to fight than to face the consequences of doing nothing.

Others, including some religious people, believe that it is never right to go to war. They are called **pacifists**.

The word *pacifist* comes from the Latin language and means *peace-maker*. The Pacific Ocean was named by an explorer called Magellan, who thought it was a calm and peaceful sea.

This sculpture, called *Non-Violence*, sits outside the United Nations headquarters in New York. It expresses a resolution of the UN General Assembly 'to secure a culture of peace, tolerance, understanding and non-violence'.

King Ashoka

Ashoka was King of India in the third century BCE. He was a vicious and bloodthirsty ruler who ruthlessly tortured and killed anyone who displeased him. He expanded his empire through bloody wars, including the conquest of Kalinga, in which over 100,000 soldiers were killed.

It is said that, after the war with Kalinga, a woman approached Ashoka and said, 'Your actions have taken from me my father, husband, and son. Now what have I left to live for?'

Ashoka returned to the battleground, and was moved by what he saw. He cried out:

'What have I done? If this is victory, what is defeat? If this is justice, what is injustice? Does it show courage to kill children and women? Do I do it to widen my empire or to destroy the other's kingdom?'

When King Ashoka returned to his palace, he was a changed man. He rejected violence in all its forms and became a Buddhist. He made Buddhism the state religion, and spent the rest of his life doing good deeds and promoting the Buddhist religion. Still today he is regarded as a model of peaceful leadership.

King Ashoka had pillars put up all over his kingdom. On these pillars, as well as on rocks and cave walls, he had **edicts** inscribed. These were statements about how he put the teachings of the Buddha into practice during his reign.

Ahimsa

Ahimsa means non-violence and is a central teaching of Buddhism. Buddhists follow moral guidelines called the **Five Precepts**. The first precept is, 'I shall avoid taking life'. Some Buddhists go further, and say that it means, 'I shall love all beings so I will not want to kill any'.

George Fox

George Fox was born in 1624 in Leicestershire. Before he was twenty years old, he came to believe that people could experience God directly and did not need priests.

Fox formed a group called the Religious Society of Friends, better known as the **Quakers**. Quaker preachers travelled the country and the organisation grew very quickly.

Quakers refused to attend services of the Church of England, and refused to pay taxes to support it. Some were arrested and imprisoned; some were shipped to America, which was then a British colony, where the Quaker movement continued to spread.

George Fox was a pacifist. When he was in prison in 1651, he was offered his freedom if he joined the army. He refused. Pacifism became an important belief for Quakers, and, in 1660, Fox and others wrote a Peace Testimony and sent it to the King. One line reads:

'All bloody principles and practices, we … do utterly deny, with all outward wars and strife and fightings with outward weapons, for any end or under any pretence whatsoever.'

Conscientious objectors

Most Quakers are **conscientious objectors**. These are people who refuse to fight in wars, even if that means breaking the law. In wartime, Quakers have set up alternatives to military service. For example, in the two World Wars, British Quakers set up the Friends' Ambulance Unit to help wounded soldiers. In 1947, the Quakers were awarded the Nobel Peace Prize for their **humanitarian** work.

Knowledge check

1 When did King Ashoka live?

2 What made Ashoka become a pacifist?

3 What does ahimsa mean?

4 When did George Fox live?

5 What is the Religious Society of Friends better known as?

6 What is a conscientious objector?

7 In which year did the Quakers win the Nobel Peace Prize?

Activity A

1 The Edicts of Ashoka described how the King ruled over his people in ways that were caring, fair and peaceful.

2 Write some statements about the things the ruler of a country should do to keep his or her subjects happy.

3 You could make a display of your ideas by making some pillars and attaching your statements to them.

4 To help you get ideas, you could read some of Ashoka's Edicts. You can find them on the Internet.

Activity B

1 Write out the script of a discussion between two Christians: one who believes in the Just War theory, and a Quaker.

2 You should try to present the points on which they might agree.

3 You should also get them to argue for their different points of view.

Activity C

1 Find out more about the Quaker movement.

2 Focus on their history, their beliefs, and how they put their beliefs into practice.

3 You could present your findings in the form of a script for a television documentary.

Activity D

'Pacifists live in a world of fantasy. There will always be wars.'

1 What reasons might some people have for saying this?

2 Why might others disagree?

3 You should refer to ahimsa and the Just War theory in your answer.

3.4 Is it ever right to kill?

Learning objectives

You will …
- find out what euthanasia and assisted suicide are
- understand reasons for and against euthanasia and assisted suicide
- understand why most religious people are against euthanasia and assisted suicide
- analyse why some people may see murder as an act of compassion.

Some people believe that, in certain circumstances, it may be right to kill a person out of **compassion** – love and kindness.

Euthanasia and assisted suicide

Euthanasia is the deliberate killing of someone who is very ill. It is done to relieve them of suffering. It is sometimes called mercy killing.

For example, a doctor who administers an overdose of a drug to end a patient's life, at their request, would be considered to have committed euthanasia.

Assisted suicide is the act of deliberately providing help to another person so that they can end their own life and so be relieved of suffering. It is sometimes called self-deliverance.

For example, if a relative of a person with an illness from which they will eventually die gives them powerful drugs, knowing that the person intends to take them to kill themselves, they would be assisting suicide.

- Euthanasia is illegal in Britain, and is regarded as either manslaughter or murder.
- Although it is not illegal to attempt to take your own life, assisting the suicide of another person is against the law.
- Eighty per cent of the UK's population believe euthanasia and assisted suicide should be allowed.

Euthanasia is an act of love and kindness.

These days there are drugs that reduce pain.

It's your life; you should be able to decide how it ends.

Human life is sacred.

It is cruel to keep someone alive and in pain when they want to die.

Quality of life is more important than the length of it.

Life is a gift from God. Only God can take it away.

It would help people to face death knowing that they could die with dignity.

Many people recover from serious illnesses, even after they have lost hope.

Taking someone's life shows that life has no value.

Everyone dies, and it doesn't matter when.

Most religious people believe that euthanasia and assisted suicide are wrong.

The person's mind may not be working properly so they can't make a good decision.

Compassionate murder

A true story

On 9 April 1945, a Christian minister, Dietrich Bonhoeffer, was executed by the Nazis. He had been arrested two years earlier for helping Jews escape from Germany to safety in Switzerland. Bonhoeffer had also been involved in a plot to kill Adolf Hitler, the leader of Germany.

How could a Christian pacifist justify murder? Dietrich explained this to his sister-in-law:

'If I see a madman driving a car into a group of innocent bystanders, then I can't, as a Christian, simply wait for the catastrophe and then comfort the wounded and bury the dead. I must try to wrestle the steering wheel out of the hands of the driver.'

Dietrich Bonhoeffer was executed for helping Jews escape the Holocaust.

A parable

The Buddha, in one of his former lives, was a sea captain. On one occasion, he led a group of five hundred merchants on an ocean voyage. The merchants were all followers of the **dharma** and were very far advanced on the path to enlightenment. A nasty criminal managed to join the voyage, with a plan to kill all of the merchants and take their wealth. But an ocean-spirit informed the future Buddha of the situation, and the future Buddha decided to kill the criminal.

Knowledge check

1 What is euthanasia?
2 What is assisted suicide?
3 Is assisted suicide legal in Britain?
4 What proportion of the UK's population support euthanasia and assisted suicide?
5 Why was Dietrich Bonhoeffer executed?
6 Who had Bonhoeffer plotted to kill?
7 Who did the future Buddha decide to kill?

Activity A

1 Look at the statements about euthanasia in the boxes on page 72.
2 Which of them support euthanasia and which are against it?
3 Sort them into two columns, headed FOR and AGAINST.
4 Try to add more statements to each column.

Activity B

1 Why do you think most religious people believe euthanasia and assisted suicide are wrong?
2 Try to find quotations from religious leaders to support your answer.
3 What is your view?

Activity C

1 If 80 per cent of people believe that euthanasia and assisted suicide should be made legal, why haven't they been legalised?
2 Do you think that parliament should take religious views into account when making laws about euthanasia and assisted suicide?
3 Give reasons and examples in your answer.

Activity D

1 Explain, in your own words, why Dietrich Bonhoeffer decided to kill Hitler.
2 From your knowledge of Buddhism, explain why the future Buddha decided to kill the criminal.
3 What are your views about Bonhoeffer's and the Buddha's reasoning?
4 You should refer to Christianity and Buddhism in your answer.

3.5 Why is there conflict in Israel/Palestine?

Learning objectives

You will ...
- understand why there is conflict between Israel and the Palestinians
- find out about the history of the conflict
- understand the part religious tradition plays in the conflict
- consider possible solutions to the conflict.

Israel and Palestine are hardly ever out of the news. There has been conflict there for over 60 years. It's not a religious conflict: it's a conflict about land. But the land itself has deep religious importance.

What's it all about?

The land in question is the Holy Land. This is the land that the Jews believe was promised to them by God. Jews sometimes call it the Promised Land. The land is important to Christians and Muslims, too.

What is the history of the conflict?

The Holy Land was Jewish territory until two thousand years ago, when the Romans killed large numbers of Jews and forced others to leave their homeland. They named it Palestine. From that time, Arabs, mainly Muslims with some Christians, became the biggest group there, while Jews settled in other parts of the world.

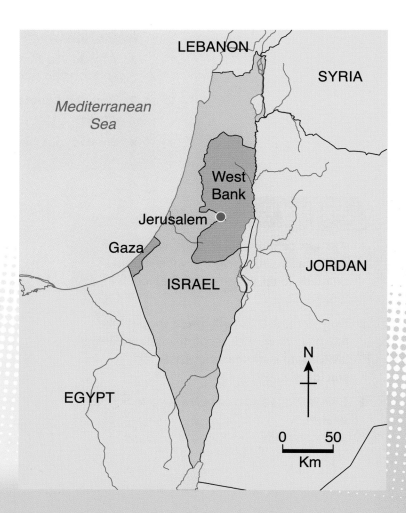

After the First World War, the British ruled in Palestine. At this time, Jews were being persecuted in Europe and Russia, and some started to move into the land they believed was theirs by right. Some Arab leaders became alarmed as the Jewish population grew, and revolted against the British. The British, in turn, restricted Jewish entry to Palestine. After the Second World War, Britain let the United Nations decide what to do with Palestine.

The United Nations decided to divide Palestine between the Jews and the Arabs. The Jews agreed and called their land Israel. The Arabs did not agree. The Arab states that surrounded the new Jewish state attacked it. When the fighting stopped, Israel had increased in size due to the new areas its soldiers had taken control over. Two areas remained under Arab control: a coastal strip around the city of Gaza (the Gaza Strip), and land to the west of the River Jordan (the West Bank). The city of Jerusalem was split: the western part going to the Israelis, and East Jerusalem to Jordanian Arabs. The Israelis captured the Gaza Strip and the West Bank, including East Jerusalem, in 1967.

Today, Israel is recognised as a Jewish state, but the Palestinians have no state of their own. There is continued conflict between the Palestinians and the Israelis.

What makes the situation so complicated?

There are a number of reasons.
- Some Palestinians refuse to recognise the state of Israel.
- Some Palestinian groups have attacked Israel and the Jewish people.
- Israel has built settlements for Israelis in the West Bank.
- Israel occupies East Jerusalem.
- Some Palestinians operate terrorist activities against the Israelis.
- Israeli soldiers are reported to have violated the human rights of Palestinians.
- Israel has restricted access to the Gaza Strip, making trade difficult for Palestinians.
- Israel has built a barrier around the West Bank.

The West Bank barrier is over 700 kilometres long. Israel says it ensures its security. The International Court of Justice says it is illegal.

What's religion got to do with it?

Although the conflict over Israel/Palestine is not a religious one, religious tradition is an important part of the identities of both Arabs and Jews, even for those who are not religious. And the land they claim and love is considered holy by most Jews, Christians and Muslims.

The Council of Religious Institutions of the Holy Land is an organisation consisting of religious leaders of the three faiths. They believe that religion has to be part of the solution to the conflict. They work together to try to achieve peace. This is their mission statement:

> 'As religious leaders of different faiths, who share the conviction in the one Creator, Lord of the Universe, we believe that the essence of religion is to worship **G-d** and respect the life and dignity of all human beings, regardless of religion, nationality and gender.
>
> 'We accordingly commit ourselves to use our positions and good offices to advance these sacred values, to prevent religion from being used as a source of conflict, and to promote mutual respect, a just and comprehensive peace and reconciliation between people of all faiths in the Holy Land and worldwide.'

Members of the Council try to bring Israelis and Palestinians to accept and respect each other. Their work includes advising government leaders about protecting the holy places of each religion from violence, holding conferences for Palestinian and Israeli educators, and monitoring negative **media** representations of any religion.

Knowledge check

1 By what other names is Israel/Palestine known?
2 Who forced the Jews from their homeland two thousand years ago?
3 What are the two main religions Palestinian people belong to?
4 Who ruled Palestine after the First World War?
5 What percentage of the Israeli population is Jewish?
6 Give one example of the work of the Council of Religious Institutions of the Holy Land.

Activity A

1 Find out about the flags of Israel and the Palestinian people: what they look like, and what the colours and shapes symbolise.
2 Make a poster of the flags with labels to show what they mean.
3 You could research symbols for peace and add them to your work.

Activity B

1 Draw a timeline of the history of Israel/Palestine.
2 Use information from these pages and your own research.
3 Use religious symbols to show events from Jewish, Christian and Muslim traditions.

Activity C

1 Why is Israel/Palestine important to a) Jews, b) Muslims, c) Christians?
2 Use information from Chapter 1.2 and this chapter.

Activity D

Some people believe the best solution to the Israel/Palestine problem is to have one state consisting of Israel, the West Bank and the Gaza Strip. All those who lived there would have equal rights.

Another solution is to have two states, consisting of a state of Palestine alongside the state of Israel.

1 Conduct some research into the one- and two-state proposals and the arguments for and against them.
2 Prepare a report on your findings. This could be a PowerPoint® presentation or an illustrated document.
3 Write a conclusion presenting your point of view.

3.6 Can terrorists be religious?

Learning objectives

You will …
- find out how some people link religion to terrorism
- understand the links between religion and terrorism
- consider whether terrorism can ever be justified
- analyse different opinions about religious terrorism.

JAPAN ARRESTS BUDDHIST FUGITIVE OVER TOKYO METRO GAS ATTACK

NORWEGIAN BOMBER SUSPECT CLAIMS TO BE A CHRISTIAN

HINDUS ARRESTED FOR THEATRE BLASTS

JEWISH SETTLER KILLS 30 AT HOLY SITE

MUSLIM TERRORISTS ADMIT TO BOMB PLOT

CANADIAN JUDGE SAYS SIKH GUILTY IN 2 BOMB DEATHS

These are newspaper headlines that have appeared over the last few years. They refer to violent attacks by religious people on members of the public.

There is no doubt that the attackers belonged to religious groups. But does any religion really teach people to terrorise, attack and kill members of the public?

'What is happening in some countries from the shedding of innocent blood and the bombing of buildings and ships and the destruction of public and private installations is a criminal act against Islam … Those who carry out such acts have deviant beliefs.'

(Muslim leaders in Saudi Arabia)

'A true Christian would not go and … shoot people … or blow up buildings. That's not what a Christian does. So just because a man claims to be a Christian, or even believes that he is a Christian, does not necessarily make him so.'

(Christian minister in Norway)

'The biggest myth about religion and violence, I believe, is that religion teaches hatred. I think the violence comes from a kind of love or desire for love for one's own group and a willingness to do whatever it takes to obtain it.'

(Ariel Glucklich, Dying for Heaven)

'Although terrorist groups emerge within particular religious contexts … no religion has ever taught their followers to commit terrorist acts.'

('Andi', Terrorism, Religion and Global Politics)

'Contrary to the popular image that suicide terrorism is an outcome of irrational religious fanaticism, suicide bombing attacks are resolutely a politically-motivated phenomenon.'

(Riaz Hassan, What Motivates the Suicide Bombers?)

Muslims flew aeroplanes into the World Trade Centre in New York on 11 September 2001. Afterwards, US President Bush said, 'The face of terror is not the true faith of Islam. That's not what Islam is all about. Islam is peace. These terrorists don't represent peace. They represent evil and war.'

So, does religion cause terrorism?

There may be a connection between religion and **terrorism** in the minds of some people, but this does not necessarily mean that religions are the cause of terrorist activity. Here are some more possibilities.

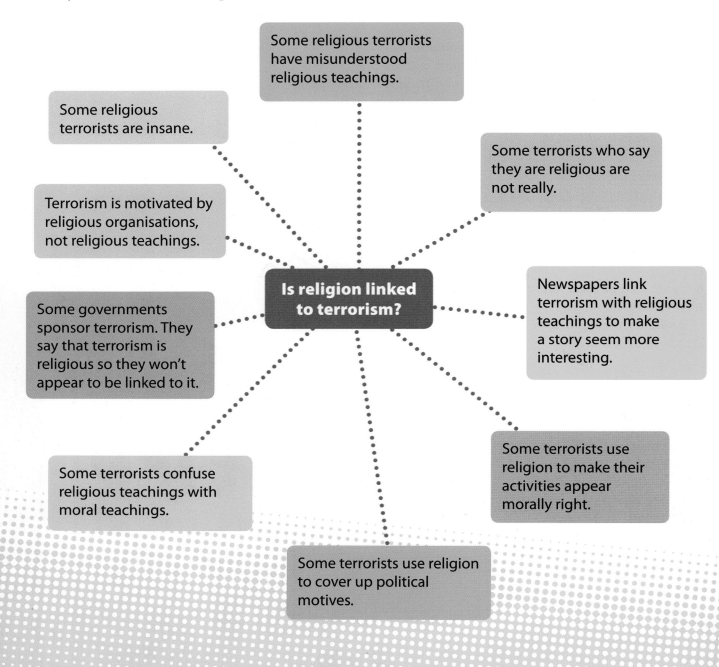

Some religious terrorists have misunderstood religious teachings.

Some religious terrorists are insane.

Terrorism is motivated by religious organisations, not religious teachings.

Some governments sponsor terrorism. They say that terrorism is religious so they won't appear to be linked to it.

Some terrorists confuse religious teachings with moral teachings.

Is religion linked to terrorism?

Some terrorists who say they are religious are not really.

Newspapers link terrorism with religious teachings to make a story seem more interesting.

Some terrorists use religion to make their activities appear morally right.

Some terrorists use religion to cover up political motives.

Knowledge check

1 What does 'terrorism' mean?
2 Give three reasons why religion may not be a direct cause of terrorism.

Activity A

1 Use the Internet to find quotations from different holy books and religious leaders about peace.
2 Write them on triangles of paper and decorate them.
3 Attach the paper triangles to a length of string to make bunting and hang them around the walls of your classroom.
4 Write a paragraph, using some of the quotations you have found, that explains what religions teach about terrorism.

Activity B

1 Revise your learning about the Just War from Chapter 3.2.
2 Could a terrorist campaign ever be called a Just War?
3 Give reasons for your answer.

Activity C

1 Explain the meanings of the quotations on page 79.
2 Which one or ones do you particularly agree with?
3 Are there any you disagree with?
4 Give reasons for your answers.
5 Use the Internet to find more views on the links between religion and terrorism.

Activity D

'There is no such thing as religious terrorism.'

1 What reasons might someone have for saying this?
2 Why might others disagree with the statement?
3 What is your view?

3.7 How is religion portrayed in the media?

Learning objectives

You will ...
- find out what the media are
- find some examples of how the media portray religion
- understand why the relationship between religion and the media is an uneasy one
- analyse the relationship between religion and the media.

What are the media?

When people talk about the media, they mean the various ways that information is communicated to a wide audience. So the term refers to television and radio, newspapers and magazines, the Internet and advertisements.

Are the media good or bad for religion?

Religions have an uneasy relationship with the media. Take *The Simpsons*. The television show portrays every aspect of ordinary life, including religion.

Most of the characters are religious and are very committed to their faith.

- Most families in Springfield, including the Simpsons, attend church every Sunday.
- Apu, the grocery store owner, is a Hindu and has a shrine to Ganesha in his shop.
- Krusty the Clown is Jewish.
- In one episode, Lisa becomes a Buddhist.

But a lot of the jokes make fun of religion and religious people.

It's no wonder that religious leaders can't agree about *The Simpsons*. One Christian minister said: 'It portrays Christians as being out of touch with reality. It makes anyone who follows God look like a fool.' Yet Rowan Williams, the former Archbishop of Canterbury, called the show 'a positive example to children' with 'a strong sense of family values'.

Non-religious people can't agree either. One atheist posted on the Internet: 'Only the good people are religious and … those who are not are immoral … I stopped watching in disgust.' While another says: '*The Simpsons* shows just how stupid religion is.'

The media can encourage stereotyping of religious individuals and groups.

The media can encourage people and communities to live together peacefully by helping people understand religious groups better.

The media can be used by religions to get their messages across to a wide range of people.

The media can be used by religions to convert people.

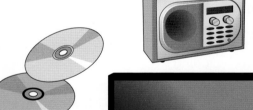

The media can combat stereotyping by providing accurate information about religions.

The media can openly ridicule or insult religious people and their beliefs and practices.

The media deliberately headline negative stories about religions to get a big response.

The media can be used by religions to teach people about their faith.

The media can encourage violence against religious groups.

The media can broadcast religious services for their members.

The media can be used to advertise religious events.

Knowledge check

1 What does the word 'media' refer to?

2 Give four examples of media.

3 How does *The Simpsons* present religion in a positive light?

4 Why might an atheist think that *The Simpsons* is against religion?

5 Why does Rowan Williams think *The Simpsons* is 'a positive example to children'?

6 How can the media encourage people to live together peacefully?

7 How can the media combat religious stereotyping?

Activity A

1 Read the statements about religion and the media in the speech bubbles on page 83.

2 Sort them into two categories: those that show the media to be good for religion, and those that show how the media can work against it.

3 Investigate various media to try to find examples in both categories.

Activity B

In 2008, writer Ariane Sherine saw an advertisement from a Christian group on a bus that read, 'When the Son of Man comes, will he find faith on this Earth?' She thought that atheists should respond by having an advertising campaign of their own. So the British Humanist Association (BHA) put posters on buses saying, 'There's probably no God. Now stop worrying and enjoy your life.' Some Christian organisations, including Christian Voice (CV), tried to stop the campaign. When their efforts proved to be unsuccessful, they began a campaign of their own, starting with a poster that read, 'There definitely is a God. So join the Christian Party and enjoy your life.'

1 Conduct some research into the bus advertising campaigns of the British Humanist Association and Christian Voice.

2 Imagine that representatives of BHA and CV are being interviewed on a television show. Write a script in which the two representatives argue against each other to support their own points of view.

3 Many Christians supported the BHA rather than CV. Why was this the case?

4 Write a series of bus advertisements to present your views about religion.

Activity C

1 On the Internet, look at some clips from *The Simpsons* that have religious themes.

2 Conduct some research into views of religious and non-religious people on religion and *The Simpsons*.

3 Do you think that the show is fair in the ways it represents religion? Give reasons and examples.

Activity D

1 Some people think that the news media in the UK have given Islam and Muslims a negative image, especially since 9/11. This is known as **Islamophobia**.

2 Find some examples of Islamophobia in British news stories.

3 From your knowledge of Islam, explain why the examples are Islamophobic.

4 Do you think the press is responsible for promoting Islamophobia in the UK?

3.8 What do the religions have in common?

Learning objectives

You will ...
- find out about the kinds of ideas that religions agree about
- understand common religious ideas
- link religious teachings to important religious ideas
- compare religious and non-religious ideas.

When we look at conflict between religious groups, it may seem as if the groups are poles apart and have no common ground. These conflicts emphasise the differences between religions.

But religions do have things they agree about. Of course, they have different ideas; but they have different ideas about the same sorts of things.

SPIRITUALITY

Religious people believe that there is more than the material world we see. They have:
- a sense of **transcendence**, when people feel a relationship with a power or powers that govern life
- **numinous** experiences, when people are moved by beauty, love or creativity
- belief that life has meaning and purpose
- belief that life does not end when the body dies.

EMPATHY

Religious people feel that individuals can share feelings with each other. They believe:
- that all beings are connected
- in the sanctity of life – that life, especially human life, has infinite value
- in compassion – an ability to understand other people's feelings and a desire to help them when they are suffering
- in service to others
- that serving others has a positive effect on their own lives.

ETHICS

Because life is sacred and all beings are connected, religions teach:
- about the importance of values, like love, justice, truth and peace
- the **Golden Rule** – that people should treat each other as they would like to be treated
- about **stewardship** – that human beings should look after the natural world around them.

A

'Just as treasures are uncovered from the earth, so merit appears from good deeds.'

(Buddhism)

B

'The soul neither dies, nor can it be destroyed.'

(Sikhism)

C

'Human life is sacred because from its beginning it involves the creative action of God.'

(Christianity)

D

'He who experiences the unity of life sees himself in all beings, and all beings in himself.'

(Buddhism)

E

'That which you want for yourself, seek for mankind.'

(Islam)

F

'You shall find peace serving others.'

(Sikhism)

G

'I look at the heavens you made with your hands, I see the moon and the stars you created, and I wonder, "Why are people so important to you? Why do you even think about them?"'

(Judaism)

H

'My heart breaks to see the sufferings of all souls.'

(Hinduism)

I

'Man's chief end is to glorify God and to enjoy him forever.'

(Christianity)

J

'Do you not see that God has made subject to you (humans) all that is on the Earth?'

(Islam)

K

'And now these three remain: faith, hope and love. But the greatest of these is love.'

(Christianity)

L

'So be humble under God's powerful hand … Give all your worries to him, because he cares for you.'

(Christianity)

Religions for Peace is an association of organisations around the world dedicated to promoting peace. Each of the organisations brings together representatives from the world's major religions. They emphasise the beliefs and values they have in common and celebrate their differences. Their aim is to tackle issues of conflict and war wherever in the world they occur.

Religions for Peace recognises that religious communities are powerful because they consist of people from different nations, cultures, and ethnic and social backgrounds. They can therefore bring people together to prevent conflict and create the conditions for peace. They have, for example, brought warring groups in Sierra Leone together for dialogue and reconciliation.

Knowledge check

1 What is a numinous experience?

2 What does empathy mean?

3 What is compassion?

4 What is the name of the idea that people should treat each other as they would like to be treated?

5 What is stewardship?

Activity A

1 Match each of the quotations on page 86 with the bullet points on page 85.

2 You could use this information to design a leaflet called One World Religion.

3 Your leaflet should aim to show non-religious people what religion is about.

Activity B

1 Read the bullet points on page 85 that describe the ideas that religions have in common.

2 Which of these ideas might non-religious people agree with?

3 Draw up a chart or diagram to show which ideas religious and non-religious people have in common, and which are unique to those who are religious.

Activity C

1 Find out more about Religions for Peace.

2 Make a PowerPoint® presentation or promotional booklet explaining why Religions for Peace was formed, and describing some of their initiatives and achievements.

3 Do you think that it is more important for religions to work together to help others than to do it individually? Give reasons for your answer and examples from your research.

Activity D

'For we know that our patchwork heritage is a strength, not a weakness. We are a nation of Christians and Muslims, Jews and Hindus – and non-believers.'
(President Barack Obama)

1 Do you agree with Barack Obama?

2 Give reasons for your answer. Make sure you refer to some of the ideas that are common to religions.

3 Why might some people have a different opinion from yours?

The big assignment

Task

To design a website for a multi-religious organisation promoting peace.

Objectives

- To know facts about some religiously motivated conflicts.
- To understand religious teachings and beliefs about violence, war and peace.
- To be able to analyse and apply religious teachings to real situations and issues.

Outcome

To produce the contents of a website (either electronically or printed out) presenting religious teachings about conflict and peace. Your work should suggest ways in which people of different faiths could work together for peace.

Guidance

1 Work in groups of six. Each member of the group should work on a different aspect of the task.

2 As a group, design a sitemap: a list of pages for the website suggesting what sort of information each page should contain.

3 Think of a name for your organisation and design a logo that could appear on each web page.

4 Group members should choose a page to work on from the following suggestions:

- home page: mission statements (what the organisation hopes to achieve) and values statements (the beliefs that the leaders of the organisation share)

- three pages covering different conflicts in which religion plays or has played a part – for example, religious conflict in history; Israel/Palestine; China/Tibet; Sri Lanka; Kashmir; religious terrorism

- a page of quotations from religious texts, religious leaders and religious writers about violence, conflict and war

- a page of suggestions as to what people could do to make lives better for people involved in conflict. This could include spiritual support (e.g. prayers), political support (e.g. protests), diplomatic support (e.g. mediation) and practical support (for example, medical aid).

5 Group members should exchange completed pages with each other for peer assessment (i.e. to discuss what could be done to improve the work).

6 The completed works could be presented as printed or written pages or PowerPoint® slides.

Assessment

You will be assessed on:

✓ how you use specialist vocabulary

✓ how you describe and explain religious conflicts

✓ how you explain religious teachings and beliefs about violence, conflict and peace

✓ how you are able to apply religious teachings and beliefs to real-life situations.

Glossary

Abrahamic faiths The religions that can be traced back to Abraham: Judaism, Christianity and Islam

Adi Granth Alternative title for **Guru Granth Sahib**

Agents of socialisation The institutions that socialise us

Ahimsa Non-violence (Hinduism, Buddhism)

Al-Quds 'The Holy'; Islamic name for Jerusalem

Altruism Putting the welfare of others before one's own

Anatta No permanent self or soul (Buddhism)

Apartheid Political system in South Africa until 1990 which separated people from different ethnic groups

Assisted suicide Helping someone end their life

Atheist A person who believes that there is no God

Bhikkhu Buddhist monk

Bhikkhuni Buddhist nun

Bishop A senior Christian leader

Brahmin Hindu caste from which religious leaders come

Compassion Feeling the suffering of others

Conscientious objector A person who will not fight in a war on principle

Cosmological To do with the universe

Dharma Teachings of the Buddha

Dukkha Suffering, unsatisfactoriness (Buddhism)

Edict A formal announcement

Enlightened Having an understanding of the truth about life

Euthanasia The painless killing of someone dying from a terminal illness

Five Precepts Moral guidelines (Buddhism)

G-d God. Often used by Jews in print in order to avoid using the word God, which is holy

Golden Rule A code that requires people to treat others as they would like to be treated

Granthi A person who is responsible for the **Guru Granth Sahib** and reads from it in services

Gurdwara Sikh place of worship

Guru Granth Sahib The holy book of Sikhism

Humanitarian Caring for others

Imam Leader of prayers (Islam)

Insha'Allah Arabic for 'God willing' (Islam)

Islamophobia A fear or hatred of Islam and Muslims

Jihad Individual spiritual effort or struggle. Also used to refer to military defence of Islam

Just War The theory that going to war may be a better option than not going to war (Christianity)

Karma Actions that have effects

Lama A Tibetan Buddhist monk and teacher

Lay Not **ordained**

Martyr A person who dies for a cause they believe is right

Media The various ways that information is communicated to a wide audience

Mendicant A religious person who owns nothing and relies on others for daily needs

Minister Someone who has been given the authority to perform certain roles within the Church

Moksha Freedom from the cycle of birth and death (Hinduism, Sikhism)

Monastery Place where **monks** and **nuns** live

Monk A religious man who devotes himself to his faith away from society (Christianity, Buddhism)

Numinous Moved by beauty, love or creativity

Nun A religious woman who devotes herself to her faith away from society (Christianity, Buddhism)

Omnipotent All-powerful

Ontological To do with existence

Ordained Appointed to do a particular job in a religious community

Pacifist A person who believes that it is never right to go to war

Pastor Alternative word for **minister**

Pilgrim Person who travels to a holy place for religious reasons

Pilgrimage Journey to a holy place for religious reasons

Predestination Advance decisions about what will happen in the future

President Lay leader of a synagogue (Judaism)

Priest An **ordained** leader of a Christian group

Puja Worship (Hinduism, Buddhism)

Quakers Religious Society of Friends

Rabbi Ordained teacher and leader (Judaism)

Sadhu Wandering holy man (Hinduism, Buddhism)

Sanctity of life The belief that life is holy and belongs to God

Sangha Community, either of **bhikkhus** or of all Buddhists

Segregate Force the separation of different ethnic groups

Sentient Having feelings

Sermon Religious talk or lecture

Shalom Hebrew word meaning 'peace', used as a greeting by Jews

Socialisation The process of learning to fit into society

Stewardship Responsibility for looking after the environment

Supernatural Above the laws of nature

Talmud Written teachings about the Jewish law

Terrorism Unlawful violence, or the threat of violence, to further a cause

Theist A person who believes that there is a God

Tirtha Pilgrimage site (Hinduism)

Torah Five books of Jewish law

Transcendence Feeling of being apart from the ordinary world

Utility Usefulness

Vihara Buddhist **monastery**

Index

Acknowledgements

The Publishers would like to thank the following for permission to reproduce copyright material:

Text credits
Scripture quotations taken from The Holy Bible, New International Version Anglicised. Copyright © 1979, 1984 by Biblica, Inc. Used by permission of Hodder & Stoughton Publishers, a division of Hachette UK Ltd. All rights reserved. 'NIV' is a registered trademark of Biblica, Inc. UK trademark number 1448790; and Zondervan Publishing House, www.zondervan.com.
p. 5 Survey statistics – Alton Towers: http://riderater.co.uk;
British Museum: http://www.britishmuseum.org/about_us/news_and_press;
Stonehenge: http://www.guardian.co.uk/culture/2012;
1066 Battle of Hastings: http://www.guardian.co.uk/news/datablog/2011;
Edinburgh Castle: http://www.guardian.co.uk/news/datablog/2011;
London Eye: http://www.londoneye.com/AboutUs/InterestingFacts;
Our Lady of Guadeloupe, Mexico: http://www.arcworld.org;
Ayyappa Saranam, India: http://www.arcworld.org;
Western Wall, Israel: http://www.arcworld.org;
Amritsar, India: http://www.arcworld.org;
Lumbini, Nepal: http://www.precioustravelsnepal.com;
Karbala, Iraq: http://www.arcworld.org

Photo credits
p.4 *l* © johny007pan – Fotolia, *r* © ramonespelt – Fotolia; **p.5** © Jupiterimages/Botanica/ Getty Images; **p.9** © Eyal Nahmias/Alamy; **p.10** *t* © Hanan Isachar/Corbis, *b* © Israel images/Alamy; **p.12** © Tim Graham/Alamy; **p.13** © Pep Roig/Alamy; **p.14** © davidevison – Fotolia; **p.16** *tl* © RIA Novosti/TopFoto, *cl* © ALLSTAR Picture Library/Alamy, *tr* © Brian J. Ritchie/ Hotsauce/Rex Features, *cr* © Monica M. Davey/epa/Corbis, *br* © Mike Webster/ Rex Features; **p.20** *c* © khunaspix – Fotolia, *l* © Sean Gallup/Getty Images *r* © RichardBaker/ Alamy; **p.22** *tl* © RichardBaker/Alamy, *tr* © Robert Sabo/NY Daily News Archive via Getty Images, *cl* © Caro/Alamy, *cr* © Art Directors & TRIP/Alamy, *b* © Sean Gallup/ Getty Images; **p.24** © Ralph Orlowski/Getty Images; **p.25** © Frank Trapper/Corbis; **p.26** © Bettmann/Corbis; **p.28** © Angelo Giampiccolo – Fotolia; **p.29** © Eddie Gerald/Alamy; **p.30** © Pascal van Heesch/Alamy; **p.32** *tl* © Tim Graham/ Alamy, *bl* © Xurxo Lobato/Getty images; **p.33** *tl* © Israel images/Alamy, *tr* © Pep Roig/Alamy, *b* © Jonathan Nackstrand/ AFP/Getty Images; **p.38** © Peter Willi/SuperStock; **p.40** *c* © Pixeltheater – Fotolia, *r* © SeanPavonePhoto – Fotolia; **p.41** *l* © Petro Feketa – Fotolia, *r* © Joanna Zielinska – Fotolia; **p.51** *t* © Whitebox Media – Fotolia, *c* © Sipa USA/Rex Features, *b* © vario images GmbH & Co.KG/Alamy, *bl* © Daniel Täger – Fotolia; **p.58 & 59** © Tom and Steve/Flickr/Getty Images; **p.60** © gregorydean – Fotolia; **p.62** © Roman Sluka – Fotolia; **p.65** © Mike Brown/Getty Images; **p.67** © SeanPavonePhoto – Fotolia; **p.68** © Nikreates/Alamy; **p.72** © The Granger Collection, NYC/TopFoto; **p.75** © paul prescott – Fotolia; **p.79** © Tamara Beckwith/Rex Features; **p.82** © c.20thC.Fox/Everett/Rex Features; **p.88 & 89** © RTimages/Alamy